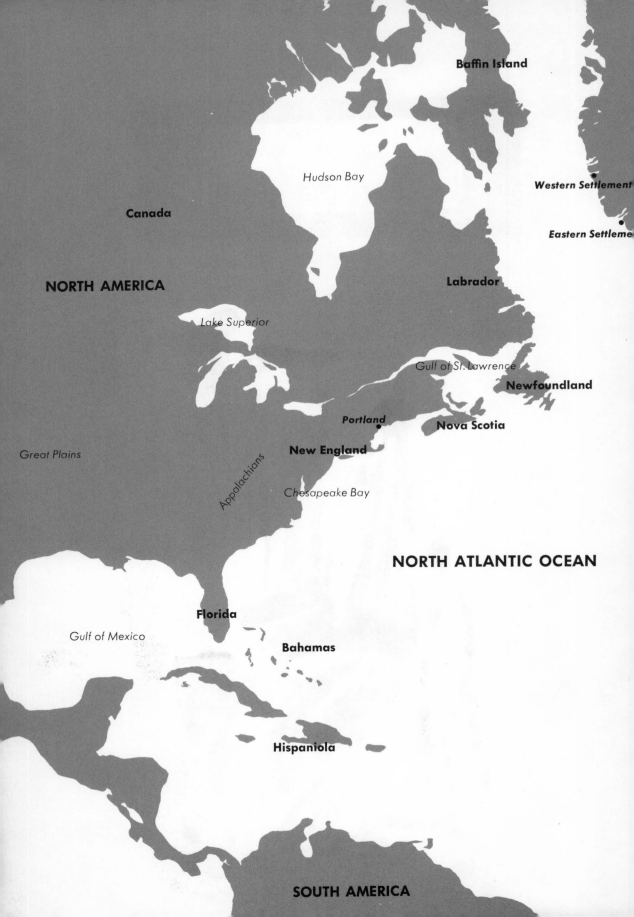

Greenland

Iceland

Norway

Sweden

Denmark

Scotland

Ireland

England

EUROPE

Bristol

France

Portugal

Spain

Sicily

Mediterranean Sea

Azores

Lisbon

Strait of Gibraltar

Canary Islands

AFRICA

Guinea

WHO DISCOVERED AMERICA?

Who were the earliest Americans? How long ago did people from the Old World first visit the New World?

To solve these mysteries, scientists and scholars study such clues as a lump of Rhode Island coal found in Greenland . . . the use of blowguns with poison darts . . . a spearpoint embedded in the bones of a long-extinct animal . . . Viking sagas of exploration and adventure . . . a parcheesi game with complicated rules . . . Peruvian mummies with silky red hair . . . weather-beaten rock carvings in old languages . . . small animal figures mounted on wheels . . . modern glass floats from Japanese fishing nets, washed up on the American shores of the Pacific.

In this surprising scientific detective story, Patricia Lauber shows how specialists investigate such clues to fill in the story of man in the New World long before the age of the great Renaissance explorers.

WHO DISCOVERED

AMERICA?

Settlers and Explorers of the New
World Before the Time of Columbus

by Patricia Lauber

Illustrated with photographs, prints, and maps

RANDOM HOUSE · NEW YORK

FRONT-MATTER ILLUSTRATIONS: Reverse of end-paper: Mosaic reproduction of Aztec carving shown on page 8. Title page: Maya stone carving from Bonampak; Norse helmet (seventh century) from Sutton Hoo; Aztec painting of Spanish conquistador. Copyright page: Norse rune stone. Contents page: Maya clay sculpture. Page vi: Norse horse brass; Norwegian carving (twelfth century). Half title: Viking ornament; Maya jade mask. Page viii: Woodcut from Columbus Letter (1493).

ACKNOWLEDGMENTS: For helpful suggestions in the preparation of this book, the author and the publisher are grateful to: Gordon F. Ekholm, Curator of Mexican Archaeology, American Museum of Natural History; Craig Fisher, producer of the documentary film *The First Americans;* Sean Morrison; Clifford Evans, Curator, Department of Anthropology, Smithsonian Institution, U.S. National Museum; and Donald Crabtree, Idaho State University.

Library of Congress Catalog Card Number: 71–99431
Manufactured in the United States of America
Printed by Rae Publishing Co., Cedar Grove, N. J.
Bound by Economy Binding Corp., Kearny, N. J.
Designed by Murray M. Herman

Contents

WHO
DISCOVERED
AMERICA?

A Puzzling Discovery

Early in the morning of August 3, 1492, three small ships set sail from Spain on an extraordinary voyage. Under the command of Christopher Columbus, they were to sail westward to the East, across the uncharted Ocean Sea. If the voyage succeeded, it would establish a direct sea route between Europe and the fabled lands of the Indies, a name then used for most of eastern Asia—Japan, China, India, Burma, and the Spice Islands.

The voyage, however, was not yet really under way. On the third day out, the *Pinta's* rudder broke, and the ships put into the Canary Islands for repairs and additional supplies. Finally, on September 6, all was again ready. The flagship *Santa María*, the *Pinta,* and the *Niña* hoisted sail and weighed anchor.

At first the winds were light and variable, sometimes dying altogether, and so for a few days the lofty mountain peaks of the Canaries remained in sight. But by the evening of September 9 the last trace of land vanished below the horizon. The three small

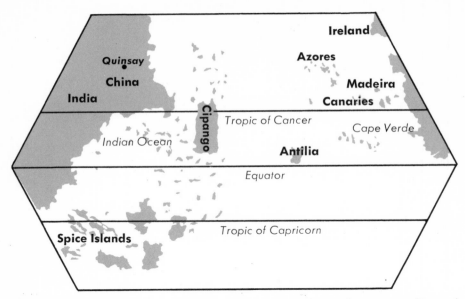

Map of Columbus' time, redrawn. Because it showed Cipango (Japan) not far from where Columbus discovered land, he was sure he had found the Indies.

ships and their ninety or so men were headed into the unknown.

A northeast trade wind filled the sails, and the ships surged ahead, following the course Columbus had given: "West; nothing to the north, nothing to the south." Now the voyage had truly begun. After years of studying and planning and searching for backers, Columbus was on his way with a fair wind and a calm sea.

In his cabin was the chart that he had drawn himself after long and careful study. Like the best maps of the day, it showed Europe, Asia, and Africa as a kind of giant island surrounded by the Ocean Sea. The chief difference between Columbus' map and others was the width of the Ocean Sea. Columbus had narrowed the distance between Europe and the East to 2,400 nautical miles.* And so, when the Canaries slipped from sight, he believed that only 2,400 miles of ocean lay between him and the nearest part of the Indies: Cipango (Japan), a land rich in gold and pearls.

___

*One nautical mile equals a little more than 6,076 feet, or about 1.2 statute miles.

As an experienced sailor, Columbus did not underestimate the sea and its dangers, but if all went well. . . .

He had no instruments to measure speed and distance, but he could estimate the speed, then calculate the distance traveled. Each day he wrote down his estimate of the ships' progress, but he kept this record secret. He gave a shortened figure to his men, thinking they might be frightened to learn how far they were from home and that they might panic if the Indies did not appear exactly where he had said they would.

For days, then weeks, they sailed on across the empty ocean. Sometimes they saw flocks of birds or the kind of cloud formations that appear over land. Yet the ocean proved as lacking in islands as it was in the sight of other sails. There was only the water, stretching on and on.

By early October it was clear to everyone that they had sailed more than 2,400 miles. There was still no land in sight, and the men were bored, restless, and fearful. Columbus himself must have known the touch of fear. By his own reckoning they had sailed far beyond the place where he had thought to find Japan. Had they somehow missed the island, and if so, where were they now?

On October 7 huge flocks of land birds passed over the ships, flying in a southwesterly direction. Columbus decided to follow the birds and ordered a change of course. During the next few days, the great flights of birds continued to pass overhead. The sight heartened the men, but even so they had had enough. By October 10 it was thirty-one days since they had seen land. Frightened to the point of becoming mutinous, they demanded that Columbus turn back.

To have come so far, to be, as the birds led him to believe, nearly in sight of land, to know that the land must be the Indies with their silks, spices, and jewels—Columbus could not turn back. He had come to find the Indies and he would find them. He quelled the mutiny and bargained with his captains for three more days in which to reach the Indies.

The next day the sea itself began to yield signs of land: branches bearing leaves and berries, a hand-carved wooden staff, a board, and still more branches. At sunset the wind rose to gale force, sending the ships racing ahead, but Columbus refused to shorten sail. Time was running out, and he wanted to make every mile possible. He signaled the other ships to keep an extra sharp watch that night.

At two o'clock in the morning of October 12, the *Pinta's* lookout cried, *"Tierra! Tierra!"* Land! Ahead of them sandy cliffs gleamed white in the moonlight, a silvery strip against the horizon.

While darkness lasted, the three ships, under shortened sail, kept their distance from the land. When daylight came, they made full sail, passed the southern tip of the island, and worked their way up the western side until they found a shallow bay. There they dropped anchor.

They had come to a small island in the group now called the Bahamas. Historians think it was the one formerly known as Watling Island and since renamed San Salvador, which was the name Columbus gave his landing place. There, together with his captains and some of the crew, Columbus knelt on the white beach to give thanks for having reached land. Rising, he named the island and claimed it for the Spanish sovereigns Ferdinand and Isabella. The date was Friday, October 12, 1492.

As Columbus had seen from his ship, there were people on the island. That did not surprise him, for he was convinced that he had reached the Indies, where he expected to meet people. What did surprise him was the appearance of these people whom he called Indians. Instead of being dressed in silken robes, they went about, Columbus noted in his journal, "as naked as when their

One of the many portraits of Christopher Columbus—all painted after his death. People who knew Columbus described him as tall, well built, with red hair (when young), blue eyes, and a hawk nose.

mothers bore them." Some painted their faces, some their whole bodies, and others only the nose. They proved to be gentle, timid people. A number had gathered at a distance to watch the Spaniards landing on the beach. Columbus made friends with them, giving some red caps and others necklaces of glass beads.

When the Spaniards went back to their ships, some of the islanders swam out, bringing parrots, skeins of cotton yarn, and other small items. The Spaniards traded trinkets such as tiny bronze bells and glass beads for these. Studying the young men, Columbus noted that they were handsome and well built, with skin that was neither black nor white and with hair that was dark, coarse, and straight, like that of a horse's tail.

For the next two days Columbus explored San Salvador, which was pleasantly green and wooded, and visited villages, where the Indians lived in huts. Through sign language he learned that there were many other islands to the south and west, and so he determined to press on. He had found land where his map showed the Indies. Therefore Japan, or perhaps China, must lie just out

Woodcuts from an illustrated edition (1493) of Columbus' report on his first voyage. Although the illustrations were not necessarily authentic, Columbus' flagship must have looked very much like the small caravel at left. Right: *Columbus and a companion landing on Hispaniola (now Haiti) in December, 1492.*

of sight. San Salvador, with its naked, gentle people, could only be an island outpost of the Indies.

As all the world knows today, Japan and China did not lie just out of sight but were another 7,000 miles away, beyond a second ocean. And so Columbus' voyage failed in its bold purpose. Yet it remains an extraordinary voyage, because its very failure led to a great age of exploration and discovery that added two whole continents to the map of the world and changed the course of history.

From the beginning there were people who suspected that the lands Columbus had found were not the Indies. The suspicion grew when Balboa crossed the Isthmus of Panama and reached the Pacific shore in 1513. It became a certainty seven years later when Magellan rounded the tip of South America and sailed across the vast sea that lay to the west of the New World. But the whole truth about what Columbus had found was slow to emerge, because it was too big to be grasped readily by men in small ships of sail. Only as explorers probed the coasts and bays and rivers, searching for a way through this great land barrier, did the truth slowly take shape: What had been found was a new world made up of two continents that stretched nearly from the North Pole to the South Pole.

But as one mystery was being solved, another was growing. Since the new lands were not part of the Indies, who were the Indians? Who were the people already living in the lands newly discovered by Europeans? The more that Europeans learned about them, the bigger the puzzle became.

For one thing, the Indians were spread throughout both continents. There were Indians in the far north, on the plains, in the woodlands, along the coasts, on islands, in the dry Southwest, in the jungles of Middle and South America, in the high mountains, and even at the cold and misty tip of South America.

For another thing, there was an astonishing variety of ways of life among the Indians. The Indians Columbus met on San Salvador were a peace-loving people who were expert fishermen and swimmers, while Indians on neighboring islands were warriors and cannibals. In the Southwest, tribes of Indians lived in large permanent villages, farmed irrigated fields, produced art, and had highly organized religious ceremonies. On the Great Plains, Indians hunted bison with bows and arrows, traveling as the bison moved and living in tepees. In other areas, small family-sized groups of Indians lived by gathering whatever food was available —bulbs, roots, seeds, fruits, grasshoppers, nuts. Coastal Indians lived by fishing. Indians of the eastern woodlands lived by hunting, fishing, and farming, and had formed a strong confederation of six tribes.

The most surprising discoveries of all were made in Mexico, Guatemala, and Peru. Here Europeans came upon three great Indian civilizations: the Aztec, the Maya, and the Inca.

The Aztecs, of central Mexico, were engineers, builders, painters, sculptors, and craftsmen. They had built a great city, with

On this massive stone carving, twelve feet across, the Aztecs recorded their view of the world. Their sun god is pictured in the center.

palaces of cut stone. They grew their food on man-made islands in a lake. They built pyramid-like temples to their gods and had a highly developed religion. They used hieroglyphics (symbols and pictures) to write on stone and on paper made from bark, had learned much about astronomy, and had developed a calendar.

The Aztec civilization was at its peak when, in 1519, Hernando Cortés began the conquest of Mexico. The Maya civilization, of southern Mexico and Guatemala, was past its height, and what the Spaniards found were the ruins of a once great civilization. The Mayas had been engineers who built stone temples, roads, and causeways. They had been skilled in the arts, mathematics, and astronomy. They had developed a hieroglyphic writing and produced books made of bark-pounded paper.

The Incas of Peru were builders of cities, roads, and bridges. They were expert farmers who terraced mountain slopes to hold the soil in place and who irrigated coastal deserts. They raised llamas and alpacas for meat and wool. Craftsmen wove fine cloth, made pottery, and smelted gold, silver, tin, and copper. Although the Incas never developed a form of writing, they were able to conquer, organize, and govern an empire that stretched nearly 3,000 miles along the western coast of South America and had a population of perhaps 16 million people. Their empire was bigger than any kingdom of Europe.

The Inca civilization was able to support full-time artists and craftsmen. This silver figure shows an alpaca, an animal raised by Inca farmers for its wool. Inca weavers used the wool for textiles whose beauty amazed the Spanish explorers.

The great Maya pyramids astonished explorers from Europe. Some thought that ancient Egyptians must have colonized Central America.

For European scholars the problem was great. Were the Indians natives of the New World and had their ancestors always lived there? If not, where had they come from?

Over the years many answers were suggested. A favorite one was that the great civilizations of the Mayas, the Aztecs, and the Incas must have their roots in Europe or the Ancient World. Learned scholars spent years trying to prove that the New World had been settled by colonists or shipwrecked sailors from ancient Egypt or Greece. The Etruscans, Phoenicians, Romans, Chinese Buddhists, and Indian Hindus were suggested as founders of these civilizations. So were the Lost Tribes of Israel, the ten tribes of the ancient Hebrew kingdom that were conquered and carried away by the king of Assyria in 722 B.C.

But if the great Indian civilizations had been founded by people from the Ancient World, then who were the other Indians? And if, as scholars thought, the Indians had been in the Americas for only 3,000 years, how was it possible that they had become so numerous and spread so far? No one answer wholly explained the puzzling discovery of the Indians.

Until fairly recent times, only a few people ever came close to the truth. These few thought that the ancestors of the Indians had come from Asia across the Bering Strait. And that is what happened, although the crossings took place much earlier than these scholars thought. The ancestors of the Indians, as modern scientists have shown, were bands of wandering hunters from Asia. The hunters walked into the New World over a now-vanished land bridge at a time when much of the Northern Hemisphere was covered by vast sheets of ice.

The First Americans

One day, thousands of years ago, a small band of hunters set out in pursuit of game. They were people who lived in northeastern Siberia, and they hunted the cold-loving mammals of the north: elk, moose, caribou, mammoths, mastodons, and other big game. This day the chase led them eastward onto a rolling plain. The plain was crisscrossed with the trails of animals that fed on its plants and drank at its ponds and lakes.

In the days, and perhaps weeks, that followed, the people continued to hunt on the plain and to move eastward across it. In time they came to a very different place, where jagged mountains soared skyward. Since the hunting was excellent, they did not turn back but stayed on in what is now Alaska. In this way, entirely by chance and with no idea that they had come into a wholly new world, these hunters became the first people ever to set foot in the Americas.

Game animals were tremendously important in the lives of all the prehistoric men who hunted them. (This cave painting is from France.)

They were followed by other bands of hunters—of men, women, and children, together with whatever possessions they had—who wandered over the same plain, came into a land that was splendid with game, and stayed. In time, the descendants of these people settled two continents.

Very little is known about these earliest Americans. But anthropologists, scientists who study mankind, think that the hunters looked much like today's American Indians, with dark, fairly straight hair, dark eyes, large brows, and large noses. The Siberian hunters were people who had left the sheltered woodlands to the south and spread across the treeless plains of a northern land. This means that they were people who had learned to live with cold and to hunt the large mammals that moved in herds

A Russian archeologist (left) and an American reporter examine an underground shelter made by prehistoric hunters in Siberia. The walls and roof were supported by the bones of mammoths.

across the plains. It shows that they were people who had developed a number of skills. They could make tools and weapons. They had learned to make shelters in the ground. They made clothing out of hides. And hunters had learned to work together as a team. A single hunter, armed with a spear, could not kill the huge, heavily furred animals of northern Siberia. A group of hunters working together could.

In many ways, these were still people who lived very simply. They knew nothing of writing. They had not yet invented the bow and arrow or the boat. They gathered and ate parts of plants, but they did not grow food. They had tamed and used no animals except perhaps the dog.

Yet they had developed enough skills to live in a cold land and hunt huge game animals. When the hunt led them eastward into a new land, the same skills served them well.

No one knows exactly when the first hunters crossed from Siberia to Alaska. But it seems certain that they came during the fourth glacial advance of the Ice Age and that the Ice Age played a major part in their coming.

An ice age is a time when sheets of ice thousands of feet thick spread out over large parts of the continents. It begins when heavy snows fall in the colder parts of the world: in polar lands and among the peaks and slopes of lofty mountains. The snows of winter are so heavy that the summer sun cannot melt them all, and so, year after year, the snow builds up. The weight of new snow packs the old into ice. These masses of ice are called glaciers.

In time, as snows fall and glaciers grow, the ice starts to flow. Giant rivers of ice reach slowly down from the mountains into the valleys. Tremendously thick sheets of ice flow out from polar lands. Then, after thousands of years have passed, a change occurs, and the glaciers start to melt and shrink. They draw back to the polar lands, back to the mountain heights, releasing great floods of meltwater.

The earth has had several ice ages. The last one, which is often called the Ice Age, began about 1.5 million years ago, and it had four main stages. Four times great glaciers advanced over the land, melted, and shrank back. The last advance started some 65,000 years ago. By 18,000 years ago nearly a third of the earth's land lay under thick sheets of ice. Then the ice began to melt. By 10,000 years ago large parts of the Northern Hemisphere were free of ice. By 6,000 years ago, the glaciers had almost shrunk back to where they are today.

An ice age has a drastic effect on ocean levels. The reason is that the oceans are the chief source of moisture for the heavy snows that fall. At a time when glaciers are growing, the snows of thousands of winters accumulate on land. With a vast quantity of

Great glaciers, remnants of the fourth advance of the Ice Age, are still to be seen today. At one time sheets of ice reached as far south as what are now the Ohio, Missouri, and Columbia rivers.

water from the oceans locked up in land ice, ocean levels drop. During the glacial advances of the Ice Age, ocean levels were several hundred feet lower than they are today. Large areas now under water were then dry land. And so it happened that a broad bridge of land linked Siberia and Alaska.

Today Alaska and Siberia are separated by the choppy waters of the Bering Strait, a narrow passage that connects the Chukchi Sea, to the north, with the Bering Sea, to the south. The strait itself is shallow, much of it less than 100 feet deep, and so are large parts of the two seas. The sea bottoms slope gently away from the strait for hundreds of miles before plunging 15,000 feet to the ocean floor. That is, in and around the Bering Strait there is a huge underwater plain, which at its widest runs 1,300 miles from north to south.

During the fourth advance of the glaciers, sea levels dropped at least 300 feet and perhaps as much as 460 feet. As a result, the plain became a huge land bridge, linking Alaska and Siberia. And like large parts of them, it was mostly free of ice. For some reason, these were not areas in which heavy snows fell and built up into glaciers. Ice covered only the mountain ranges, and these glaciers did not grow enough to reach down from the mountains and cover the surrounding land.

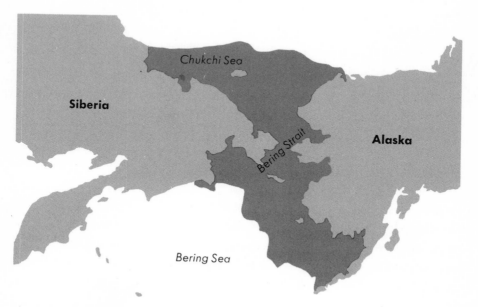

At a time when the ocean level was much lower than today, great herds of game wandered back and forth across the Bering land bridge.

The ice-free bridge was a fairly flat, low-lying land, dotted with lakes and ponds. Its plant life consisted of mosses, grasses, dwarf birch, alders, willows, and low bushes, and these were food for the browsing and grazing mammals of the north. Great herds of them wandered back and forth across the land bridge. And in time they were followed by the hunters to whom they were food and clothing.

Earth scientists are not certain of the periods when the land bridge was large and dry. They are not sure when sea levels first dropped enough to expose the plain. And they do not know how often parts of it "rose and sank" as sea levels changed.

There is, however, strong evidence that the land bridge was mostly dry from at least 25,000 years ago until about 12,000 years ago. By then the last major advance of the ice had ended, and a rise in world temperatures hastened the melting of glaciers, pouring floods of water into the oceans. The bridge may have been dry again for a brief time about 10,500 years ago. But after that the land link was cut, and hunters could no longer wander across the Bering Strait by chance. People such as the Aleuts and the Eskimos, who were late arrivals, came by boat or crossed on the winter ice, making the crossing for a purpose.

The timetable of the Ice Age and the land bridge does not tell when the earliest hunters crossed from Siberia to Alaska, but it does tell when they could have. Bands of hunters could have crossed at least 25,000 years ago and perhaps much earlier. It seems likely that large numbers of people were crossing between 20,000 and 18,000 years ago, because at that time the glacial advance was at its height and the land bridge at its biggest.

The difficulty in discovering when the first hunters arrived in Alaska lies in finding and dating traces of them. These were people who made shelters or lived in caves. They had fire. They made and used, and also broke and lost, weapons and tools. They

Many large mammals hunted by prehistoric North Americans are extinct today. But the caribou survives in Alaska and northern Canada.

skinned or butchered large animals, leaving bones or whole skeletons. They themselves died of natural causes or were killed in hunting accidents. They must therefore have left traces of their presence in the places where they lived and hunted. But so far none of these traces have been found in Alaska, and the chances that they will be are not very good.

One reason is that the sea now covers most of the places where such traces of the very earliest Americans might be found. The land bridge lies under water. So do the areas where these people hunted in Alaska. In the beginning, at least, they would have hunted along the grassy coastal plains on which herds of animals could be seen from afar. The sea has long since drowned these plains.

Another reason is that the tools and weapons of the hunters may have been so simple and crude that they would be hard to recognize as such. If the spearheads, knives, and scrapers were roughly shaped pieces of stone, they would look much like stones shaped

Modern painting of prehistoric mastodons, bison, and horses in the Mississippi Valley near the end of the Ice Age.

by natural causes. It would be almost impossible to be sure that they had been shaped by human hands.

The only thing that is certain is that the earliest Americans began arriving thousands of years before the seas rose and covered the land bridge.

For a long time Alaska was probably home and hunting ground to these people, who are known as Paleo-Indians, meaning "early or old Indians." The hunting was good. There were not very many people. And the way east or south was blocked at first by towering sheets of ice.

When there is plenty of food and living space, populations tend to grow rapidly. So the Paleo-Indians must have started to spread out, following the game trails along the foothills of the Alaskan mountains. As each band moved into new territory, its numbers again increased, and in time the Indians spread out of Alaska. Some may have made their way southward along the coast. But the main route was through the interior.

In western Canada there was a place, along the Mackenzie Valley, where two large sheets of ice met. During the times when glaciers were shrinking a little, the ice sheets pulled away from each other, and an ice-free corridor opened up. It led the mammals and men who followed it to the eastern Rockies and the Great Plains.

The plains were then very different from the dry tableland that they are today. They were wet with rivers and lakes and marshes and green with tall, thick grasses. And they were a grazing ground for herds of huge Ice Age mammals.

The herds had worn down trails that led to watering places and to other feeding grounds. The hunters followed the trails. One trail led to another and that one to still another, and so bands of hunters wandered on and on in various directions. Some went eastward, probably following the river valleys. Some went westward through ice-free passes in the Rockies. Others traveled southward, drawn on by the promise of food.

There is no way of telling how far any one band of Indians traveled, but their wandering life went on for generations and it spread the Paleo-Indians over two continents. By 11,000 years ago they had reached the tip of South America. There is evidence, dating from that time, of people who lived in a cave in southernmost Chile, eating horses and camels and cooking their meat over an open fire.

The evidence consists of bones and of charcoal from ancient fires. Scientists can find out how long ago the fires burned and the meat was cooked by a method called radiocarbon, or carbon-14, dating. It measures the amount of carbon-14 that is left in an object that was once living matter, such as some teeth or a piece of wood. From that measurement it is possible to calculate how long ago the animal or plant died.

HOW CARBON-14 DATING WORKS

Carbon-14 is a radioactive variety of the element carbon. It forms in the atmosphere, and all living things contain small amounts of it. Plants take it in when they absorb carbon dioxide from the atmosphere. Animals take it in when they eat plants or when they eat other animals that eat plants. As long as a plant or animal lives, it continues to take in carbon-14. When it dies, it ceases to do so.

As is true of all radioactive elements, the atoms of carbon-14 keep breaking down and radiating, or giving off, tiny particles. Because they are giving off particles, the atoms themselves are changed. They are no longer atoms of carbon-14 but atoms of a different sort.

The rate of breakdown of a radioactive element is measured by its half-life. The half-life of carbon-14 is about 5,700 years. This means that 5,700 years after an animal or plant has died, it contains only half the carbon-14 atoms that were present at the time of death. In the next 5,700 years, half of those atoms break down; that is, after 11,400 years have passed, only a quarter of the carbon-14 atoms remain. After 17,100 years have passed, only an eighth of them are left, and so on.

When scientists wish to date an ancient fire, they analyze the charcoal to find out how much carbon-14 it contains. They know how much carbon-14 there is in wood from a living tree, and they assume that the ancient tree contained the same amount when it was alive. They can therefore calculate how long the carbon-14 has been breaking down. For example, if the charcoal contains one quarter of the amount of carbon-14 found in a living tree, then the charcoal comes from a tree that died about 11,400 years ago. The date of the ancient fire made with that wood is roughly the same.

Carbon-14 can be used for dating up to about 50,000 years ago. If a plant or animal died before that, there is too little carbon-14 left for accurate measurement.

This method of dating is one of the most useful tools that scientists have for exploring the past, but it cannot be relied on in every case. For instance, scientists must be careful that the sample they are dating has not been affected by water. If carbon-14 has been leached out of it by water, the sample will seem to be older than it really is. Also, it is not always possible to date a find by carbon-14. Bones, for example, do not absorb much carbon-14, and they are difficult to date. Yet they are found much more often than teeth and tusks, which do absorb carbon-14 and which make excellent samples for dating.

Because of these and other problems, scientists often disagree about the accuracy of carbon-14 dates. They are most likely to accept dates that are supported by other evidence from studies of the earth, ancient climates, and ancient plants and animals. Even so, carbon-14 dating has done more to answer the question "When?" than any other method scientists possess. And it indicates that the earliest Americans arrived a very long time ago.

Today we know that these earliest Americans were hunters of large mammals, because traces of the Paleo-Indians are always found with or near the bones of mammoths, mastodons, big-horned bison, camels, horses, and other mammals that flourished in North America toward the end of the Ice Age. But these traces were a very long while coming to light.

In the early part of this century most scientists thought that people had reached the Americas only about 3,000 years ago, because they had found no traces of earlier people. They had found the remains of many mammals that died out 7,000 to 10,000 years ago, at the end of the Ice Age. But nowhere did they find signs that men had hunted these mammals.

The first major find of this kind was made only in 1926. It was made near Folsom, New Mexico, by a cowpuncher who saw something odd and wondered what it was.

Remains of a mastodon found in 1907 in New York State and reconstructed at the American Museum of Natural History. At the time, most scientists believed that such animals died out before people arrived in America.

The Search for Early Americans

One spring day in 1926 a cowpuncher from a ranch near Folsom was riding the range in search of some lost cattle. In late afternoon he was passing an arroyo, a dry gully carved in the earth by runoff from heavy rains, when his eye was caught by a line of white bones showing through the dirt of the far bank. The sight of bleached bones on the range is a familiar one to cattlemen, but the odd thing about these bones was that they lay some twenty feet below the surface.

Curious, the cowpuncher swung off his horse and went to investigate. The bones were huge, much bigger than those of cattle, and buried among them were several things that glittered. These proved to be pieces of flint that had been shaped into points, yet they did not look like any Indian arrowheads he had ever seen. He slipped a few into a pocket and rode on.

The cowpuncher did not know what he had found, except that it was something out of the ordinary. So he talked about his dis-

covery to people in Folsom, and in this way his find came to the
attention of archeologists and other scientists who study the past.
The find stirred tremendous excitement. The bones were those of
a straight-horned bison, a kind of mammal that died out about
10,000 years ago. Mixed in with these ancient bones were flint
spearpoints made by men who had hunted and killed the bison.
This was the first solid evidence of ancient hunters ever found in
the Americas. The hunters were named "Folsom men" for the
place where they were discovered.

Extensive and careful digging in the Folsom area turned up
skeleton after skeleton of straight-horned bison, sometimes with a
flint point embedded in the bones. A few of the skeletons were
lacking a leg, as though a hunter had hacked off a joint for meat.
Most, however, lacked only the tail bones, which indicates that
they were killed for their skins. (When an animal is skinned, the
tail goes with the hide.) Further evidence of skinning was found
among the pieces of flint. Some were scrapers, used for dressing
hides once the skins were stripped from the bison. If Folsom men
killed for hides alone, scientists reasoned, then they must have

Left: *New Mexico arroyo where a cowboy came upon the first trace ever found of ancient hunters in America.* Below: *The Folsom discovery—bones of a straight-horned bison found with the flint point (at lower right) of the spear used by an early hunter.*

wanted the hides for a purpose. Probably they used hides for clothing and perhaps also for making a warm bed on a pile of leaves or branches.

The ground itself added to the picture of the hunt. Below its modern surface were layers of long-dried-up mud and lines of dark soil, the kind that is rich in decayed vegetable matter. From this evidence it was clear that the region had once been much wetter than it is today. At one time the land had been threaded with rivers and gleaming with lakes and ponds. The bison skeletons were found around the edge of what had been a small lake or a pond. Coming to drink, the bison had been ambushed and killed by Folsom hunters.

The traces of rivers and lakes, together with the straight-horned bison, placed Folsom man in time. He had lived during the fourth glacial period of the Ice Age, a time when the climate of New Mexico was wet. And he had lived at least 9,000 or 10,000 years

An ingenious scientist at Idaho State University has taught himself to fashion flint tools like those of Folsom man.

ago, since he had hunted and killed straight-horned bison.

The find also showed that Folsom men were hunters of considerable skill and strength, because it would be no simple matter to attack and kill a huge, thick-skinned bison with flint-tipped spears. In addition, these people were highly skilled at flint chipping, for the spearpoints were beautifully made. First a three-inch-long piece of flint was flaked to a pointed shape. Then on each side two long grooves were delicately struck out, reaching from near the point to the base. Finally, Folsom man carefully sharpened the edges by removing tiny chips and ground the base smooth. The finished point was bound tightly to a straight shaft of wood to make a spear or dart.

The first discovery of Folsom points was followed by many others. The points were so distinctive in their workmanship that they could be recognized by almost anyone who had ever seen a drawing or photograph of them.

Since 1926 dozens of Folsom campsites have been found. Some are places where Folsom men apparently killed a mammoth or a bison and camped for a few days. Some are places where people stayed for perhaps months at a time. Here scientists have found the remains of ancient fires, scattered bones that were tossed away when the people finished their meal, and a variety of tools. They have found flint scrapers and flint knives. They have found bones that were worked by hand into some sort of tool. And they have found small pieces of flint that were shaped to needle-like points. No one is sure what these tools were used for. Perhaps they were used for making holes in the edges of skins, although so far there is no evidence that Folsom women knew how to sew. Another possibility is that they were used for tattooing, which is probably a very old form of human decoration.

One of the biggest Folsom campsites was found during the early 1930's near Clovis, in eastern New Mexico. In Ice Age times, Clovis was a wet and grass-covered region, where herds of mammals gathered to graze and to drink at its lakes.

It was obvious that Clovis had been an excellent place to hunt, because there were large collections of bison, mammoth, horse, and camel bones. It was equally clear that the Clovis campsite had been used over a long period of time, because the bones and flint points occurred in layers. This is the kind of thing that happens when generation after generation of people live in the same place. They throw away bones, broken tools, and other things that they are through with. These things get mixed in with dirt, dust, stones, and decaying vegetable matter, and so the rubbish becomes layered, with the most recent on top and the oldest at the bottom.

Clovis had several layers of rubbish. As archeologists dug down through the layers, they came upon flint points that had not been made by Folsom men. These points were about three to four

inches long, about an inch wide, and thin. Each had a groove that ran forward from the base on each side. They were much more crudely made than the Folsom points, and the cruder workmanship spoke of an earlier people. But the real proof was that these Clovis points, as they are called, were found below the Folsom points. The men who made these points had been using this campsite and hunting ground for hundreds of years before the Folsom people. Like the Folsom hunters, they were Paleo-Indians, but the Clovis hunters were of an earlier culture.

The Clovis culture, as other finds showed, was extremely successful and widespread. Many Clovis campsites and butchering sites have been found in North America, most of them dating to 12,000 or 14,000 years ago. Clovis points and other tools have been found from coast to coast and from Alaska south into Mexico.

Clovis hunters seem to have specialized in mammoths. Their points are almost always discovered along with the bones of mammoths, although sometimes the bones of bison and horses are also found. Many of the bones and skeletons are those of young mammoths, which indicates that the Clovis hunters had learned to cut the young out of the herd and to kill them instead of the more fearsome adults.

In 1936, a few years after the discovery of the Clovis hunters, a student from the University of New Mexico was exploring caves in the Sandia Mountains near Albuquerque. From the floor of one he collected a boxful of litter—bits of pottery, fragments of woven baskets, a piece of deer antler—and took them to the university museum. These odds and ends indicated that Pueblo Indians of the past few hundred years had sometimes used the cave as a stopping place during hunting trips.

The objects were not themselves of any particular interest, but the fact that the cave had been occupied by people was of great interest. Perhaps people had been using this same cave for thou-

Archeology students from the University of New Mexico working in a Sandia cave. They wear masks as protection against dust.

sands of years. Archeologists from the university decided to investigate the cave, which was shaped like a tunnel in the limestone cliff. They crawled in and, within a few hundred yards, made their first discovery: something that felt like a large curved bone. Seen in daylight, it proved to be the claw of a giant ground sloth, a huge lumbering mammal that died out toward the end of the last glacial advance. If the cave had yielded remains of an Ice Age mammal, would it also yield signs of Ice Age man? The archeologists decided to dig and find out.

Digging, as archeologists do it, is slow work, for they must be very careful not to break what lies hidden in the earth and not to disturb the order or positions in which things are found. The dig-

The Search for Early Americans   33

SANDIA   CLOVIS

ging at Sandia cave went on for several seasons. First the diggers worked their way through fairly modern dust, rubble, and bat droppings, finding traces of Pueblo Indians of 500 and 600 years ago. Then they came upon a layer of hard crust that had been formed by the action of water seeping through limestone. The water, carrying lime in solution, had dripped and spread over the cave floor. When the water evaporated, the lime was left and it hardened into a crust. The thickness of the crust showed that it had built up over a long period of time.

Such a crust could have formed only at a time when this part of New Mexico was dripping wet. This meant that the crust had formed during the last wet period of the Ice Age. Whatever lay beneath it must date from Ice Age times.

Chipping carefully through the crust, the diggers came to an ancient cave floor. There they found the bones of horses, bison, camels, and mammoths; many of the bones had been split, as if to get at the marrow. There were mammoth teeth and tusks. There were bits of charcoal from fires. Clearly, the cave had been inhabited by Ice Age men for many, many years. What men were they? A number of flint points, knives, and other tools supplied the answer. Folsom man had lived in this cave, gone out to hunt from it, brought home great chunks of meat and bone, cooked these over a cave fire, and tossed the bones into the back of the cave.

Digging down beyond the Folsom cave floor, archeologists came to a layer of yellowish, earthy clay that had been laid down by water. Beneath that they came to still another cave floor littered with the bones and teeth of horses, camels, bison, mammoths, and mastodons. There were fireplaces outlined with rounded rocks and containing bits of charcoal.

Spear points made by early American hunters of three different cultures. Folsom points varied in length from less than an inch to more than four inches.

FOLSOM

At first this cave floor looked much the same as the Folsom floor. Here ancient hunters had sat by a fire cooking meat, splitting bones for their marrow, and throwing away what they did not want. A closer look showed that these hunters had not been Folsom men. The flint spearpoints on this cave floor were totally different from the Folsom points. These Sandia points, as they were named, were roughly leaf-shaped, with a notch at one side of the rounded base. Although the hunting life of the Sandia people must have been much like that of the Clovis and Folsom people, Sandia man was earlier. He had hunted these valleys and cooked, eaten, and slept in this cave long before Folsom man. The evidence was in the layering of the floor and the cruder shaping of the flint points.

The first dating of Sandia man was done through geology. The cave had had wet periods and dry periods, and these were most likely related to the growing and melting of glaciers. When glaciers were growing and huge masses of ice covered most of the Rocky Mountains, the climate in New Mexico was wet. When glaciers were melting and shrinking, the climate was dry.

Comparing the evidence of the cave floors with what they knew about the growth and melting of glaciers, geologists concluded that Sandia man had lived in the cave about 25,000 years ago, while the Folsom people were there about 12,000 years ago.

More recently carbon-14 dating has been used on mammoth teeth and tusks from the cave. It dates the Sandia people as having lived there between 24,000 and 28,000 years ago. Some archeologists, however, think that water leached carbon-14 from the teeth and tusks and that these dates are too old.

So far only a few other Sandia sites have been found. Carbon-14 dating of charcoal, teeth, and tusks from them indicates that they are 11,000 to 16,000 years old. When more Sandia sites are found, it should be possible to date these people more exactly.

The Sandia cave was a doubly important find. It produced evidence of a culture that was even earlier than Clovis or Folsom. And it partially answered a question that had been bothering archeologists: Did the Paleo-Indians use any kind of shelter?

In Europe and many parts of Asia, early man lived in caves. Scientists have found caves in Europe that were inhabited fairly steadily for thousands of years. But until the discovery in the Sandia Mountains, no trace of American cavemen had been found. The Clovis and Folsom campsites all lay along the edges of lakes, marshes, and rivers. It seemed unlikely that Ice Age Americans had lived without shelter, relying only on campfires and hides to warm them when cold wet winds blew off the ice. At the same time, no trace of shelters had been found.

The Sandia discovery showed that if caves were available, the Paleo-Indians lived in them. What did these wandering hunters do when there were no caves? The answer to that question was not found until 1966, and it was discovered in a modern real-estate development.

In the early 1960's, a group of big real-estate projects had been started west of Albuquerque. As bulldozers and road scrapers stripped away the topsoil, they laid bare the land surface of the Ice Age. The first things to come to light were some Folsom points.

Working together, archeologists and the developers discovered the biggest known hunting area of the Ice Age, a series of campsites that stretches for some forty miles along the plains. Here at what is now Rio Rancho Estates, a graduate student from the University of New Mexico discovered that Folsom people had built and lived in tents, or lodges. The traces in the earth are clear. Each shelter was circular, about fifteen feet in diameter, and built of a framework of poles. The framework was probably covered with bison skins. An open door faced south to gather the sun's heat. Pieces of charcoal show that cooking fires were built outside.

This big discovery in New Mexico may one day give us a detailed picture of how Folsom people lived. So far, it has filled in an important gap in that picture by proving that the Paleo-Indians of the Ice Age could and did make shelters of their own.

It is not surprising that traces of these shelters are scarce, for wood and skins decay and vanish into the soil. What is both surprising and somewhat puzzling is that so few skeletons of the earliest Americans have been found. Over the years tons of animal bones have been found at the campsites and butchering sites of the Paleo-Indians, but not even one human bone has turned up at these sites. Hunting huge, horned mammals on foot and attacking them with spears must have been a dangerous occupation that brought death to many of the hunters. Yet their bones have not been found with the animal bones.

What did the Paleo-Indians do with their dead—bury them, cremate them, leave them where they fell? If the Indians buried or cremated their dead, that would help to explain why so few skeletons have been found, but most archeologists think that burial and cremation were later cultural developments. If the dead were left where they fell, then it is possible that many skeletons have been found but not recognized. The Paleo-Indian skulls that have been identified look like those of modern Indians. Two of the most important finds were recognized for what they were only because the Paleo-Indians had died suddenly in Ice Age accidents.

Some 12,000 to 16,000 years ago, for example, an Indian drowned along the swampy edge of the large lake that then filled much of the Valley of Mexico. Exactly what happened to him is not clear, but he somehow became mired in the mud, fell on his face, and died. In 1949 his skeleton was found near the village of Tepexpan. In appearance the skull and the rest of the skeleton could have been those of a modern Mexican. But in the same late Ice Age lake bed were the skeletons of two mammoths, possibly the very ones he had been hunting, which had also become mired in the mud and died. Stone knives and points were found nearby among the remains of other mammoths that had been killed and butchered.

In 1953 an oil worker near Midland, Texas, found fragments of a human skull that had been buried deep in the earth. Flint points were found nearby. When the fragments of skull were pieced together, they formed the head of a woman, which was modern in form, with fine features, small jaws, and small teeth. Archeologists imagine that this Ice Age woman was following her husband on a hunt when some sort of disaster overtook her. Possibly the same disaster overtook her husband and the rest of the band, or perhaps she was the only victim and they left her where she fell. Various attempts to date the Midland woman have produced a wide range of possibilities. She may have died anywhere from 8,000 to 20,000 years ago.

So far, archeologists have found about thirty Paleo-Indian skulls. One, which was discovered near Laguna Beach, California, has been dated by carbon-14 analysis as 17,000 years old. If the date is accurate, this Paleo-Indian, who was probably a woman, is one of the earliest yet discovered.

Another early American is Marmes man, whose remains were discovered in the state of Washington and named after the owner of the ranch on which they were found.

The first traces of Marmes man were discovered in a cave near the meeting place of the Palouse and Snake rivers. In 1962 archeologists had started to dig in this area, because they thought peo-

Display in Mexico City of the skeleton of an Indian who died at least 12,000 years ago. Found near the modern village of Tepexpan, this is one of the very few Paleo-Indian skeletons yet identified.

ple had lived there for a very long time. Also, they knew that within a few years the area would be drowned when water backed up from a dam being built on the Snake River. The shallow cave, which was really just a rock shelter, proved extremely promising. It contained layer upon layer of human remains.

The diggers soon came to a layer of volcanic ash with a human skeleton beneath it. A geologist identified the ash as having come from the volcanic eruption that formed Crater Lake, in Oregon, about 6,700 years ago. Since the skeleton was under the ash, it had to be at least 6,700 years old. By the end of the first season of digging, archeologists had found the remains of eleven ancient people who had lived in the cave 7,000 to 8,000 years ago. Some had been buried with a ceremony that included a fire and the placing of grave goods with the body. For example, the diggers found the grave of a baby who had been buried under earth and

Archeologists at work at the Marmes dig. Left: *Excavating large bones.* Right: *Sorting dirt for tiny bones. By identifying the animals that lived in a particular time and place, scientists can tell whether the climate was warm or cold.*

stones with five matched knife blades beside his body, presumably for use in an afterlife.

Later seasons of digging brought the archeologists to the bottom of the rock shelter. There they found pieces of human bones, which were named Marmes man.

Once they had assembled and examined his bones, scientists decided that this Marmes man had been about twenty years old at the time of his death. He was probably a wandering hunter who lived by fishing and by hunting elk and perhaps mammoths. No one knows how he died, but scientists were surprised to note that some of his bones were charred and split lengthwise, which suggests that he may have been cooked and eaten by his neighbors.

Carbon-14 dating indicates that this Marmes man lived between 10,000 and 11,000 years ago. The same figure was arrived at by a geologist who studied layers of material in the rock shelter and dated them from various geologic events. He thinks it possible that much earlier people may also have lived in this area. But traces of them must have been washed away by great Ice Age floods that surged across the Columbia Plateau 18,000 to 20,000 years ago and carved the present-day Palouse Canyon. The same flood turned the canyon of the Snake River into a lake. Only when the lake drained away, some 12,000 to 13,000 years ago, could people have moved into the rock shelter.

Having finished in the cave, the diggers turned to the river flood plain below the rock shelter. Here they made an even more exciting discovery. They found the bones of still other Marmes people and evidence of a campsite. They found a hearth that they think may have been used for cremating the dead. They found the bones of an elk on which the people must have fed and which was considerably larger than today's elk. They found scrapers and pieces of a bone spearpoint. And they found a bone needle. The needle is about an inch long and slender, which indicates that it was used for making fine stitches and sewing tight seams.

The Marmes people who moved into the rock shelter between 11,000 and 13,000 years ago were far from being the earliest Americans. But they are among the earliest reliably dated Americans. And so we know, among other things, that they, like the Folsom people, lived at a time when glaciers were melting and shrinking. A great change was taking place, and a way of life that had developed over thousands of years was about to come to an end.

Changing Times, Changing Ways

Because very few skeletons have been found, the earliest Americans are strangely shadow-like. We know that they came from Siberia during the Ice Age and spread through the Americas as bands of wandering hunters of big game. But while there are many samples of their tools, weapons, and fires, there are few of the hands that chipped the flint or built the fires. We know what animals they hunted, how they hunted, and how they butchered. But what we have is the remains of the animals and not of the hunters.

The weapons and the animal remains show that the Paleo-Indians had perfected the skill of big-game hunting and brought it to a fine art. Armed only with flint-tipped spears and perhaps a hand-held device called a spear thrower, they stalked and ambushed some of the world's giant mammals. Yet this was a way of life that was doomed. About 10,000 years ago a great change began to occur, and it brought to an end the age of the big-game hunters.

Reconstruction of a spear (right) and spear thrower (left) of the ancient hunters. Like a baseball bat or tennis racket, the spear thrower enables a human being to propel an object harder and faster than with his arm alone.

The change was a change in climate.

For thousands of years sheets of ice a mile or more thick had covered large parts of North America. In the interior of the continent—on the Great Plains and in the Southwest—they had created a climate that was generally cool and wet. The Ice Age was a time of cloudy skies, heavy rains, and wet snows. This climate was ideal for the herds of big grazing mammals, because grasses and other plants grew thick and green and the many shallow lakes served as watering places. Because it was ideal for the mammals, it was also ideal for the men who lived by hunting mammals. Game was plentiful and it was easy to find.

When the ice began to melt and shrink back, the climate changed. Skies cleared, temperatures rose, and heavy rains ceased to fall. As a result, shallow lakes evaporated and the rich supply of plants that had covered the grazing grounds began to thin out.

By 7,000 years ago, the period of great change had come to an end, and the climate and land were much as they are today. The age of big-game hunting had also come to an end, for the great herds of Ice Age mammals had vanished from the land. The cause of their disappearance is one of the mysteries of the Ice Age.

For many thousands of years, and long before the first men arrived, North America was inhabited by a splendid variety of mammals: by mammoths and mastodons, horses, camels, several kinds of bison, giant ground sloths, giant armadillos, tapirs, and many other kinds of now-vanished mammal. The La Brea tar pits of California have yielded the remains of thirty-five kinds of mammal that lived 15,000 years ago; by 6,000 years ago every one of the thirty-five kinds was extinct.

What happened? No single answer seems to solve the mystery.

For example, changes in climate and food supplies must have played a part in the disappearance, but they cannot be the whole answer. The Ice Age had four main stages; four times glaciers grew for thousands of years and then melted away. Many of these kinds of mammal had survived the end of earlier stages. Why did they not survive the end of the fourth? Then, too, the changes that took place in North America also occurred in Europe and Asia. Since horses and camels survived in Eurasia, why were they wiped out in North America?

Perhaps disease played a part. But it is hard to explain how disease could have wiped out some kinds of bison and not others.

Perhaps man the hunter was himself to blame. It is hard at first to believe that small bands of men, traveling on foot and carrying spears, could have wiped out such huge numbers of mammals. Yet there are reasons for thinking that man may have done just that.

One reason is that man was a newcomer to North America. When the third glacial advance ended, there were no people in the New World. By the time the fourth advance ended, North America was peopled by highly skilled hunters.

Another possible reason is that toward the end of the Ice Age, hunters may have discovered the stampede. If so, they were able to kill a whole herd of mammals by stampeding it over a cliff. Probably they started and directed the stampede by setting grass fires that drove the herd toward a cliff. Near Plainview, Texas, for example, an Ice Age kill of about a thousand bison has been found at the bottom of a cliff. Only those that fell last had to be killed with spears. The others died in the fall.

A number of scientists think that this hunting technique tipped the balance and led to the wiping out of the great herds of mammals that once roamed North America. They think so because the

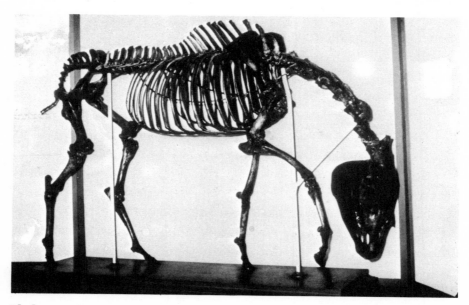

Skeleton of an Ice Age horse found in La Brea tar pits. Horses, which died out in America thousands of years ago, were reintroduced by the Spanish explorers about 450 years ago.

stampede would have come into use just at the time when changing climate and food supply placed the mammals under great stress. But other scientists do not agree with this idea. They think the human population was far too small to have had such a great effect.

Whatever happened, one thing is clear. As the ice melted and the climate changed and the great herds dwindled, a whole way of life began to change. For a time some bands of men could go on hunting big game, but others were forced to become hunters and gatherers of whatever foods they could find—small mammals, birds, shellfish, fish, insects, wild plants, nuts, seeds, berries.

This new way of life, which is called Archaic, meaning "old," was a much more local one. Ice Age hunters had moved around a great deal, because their food supply moved around. Archaic people tended to stay in one area, because their food supply stayed there. Small mammals, such as squirrels or raccoons, have a home territory; they move about within it, but they do not roam miles and miles away from it. A nut tree is rooted to the ground. Fish are found at certain places along a river.

In turning to these new sources of food, the Archaic people were forced to make a number of inventions. A flint-tipped spear might be useful for hunting deer, but it was little help to a man who was hunting squirrels, fishing, or gathering berries. By trial and error, the Archaic people developed a number of devices for collecting food. They invented fish spears. They invented snares for trapping small mammals and birds, as well as the dart, which they used for bringing down small game. They made baskets for collecting berries, nuts, seeds, and roots. They discovered how stones could be used for milling and grinding plant foods.

The Archaic culture did not spring into existence overnight. Rather, it developed slowly from ways of life that already existed. The Paleo-Indian big-game hunters had made some use of plant foods. And even before the climate changed, a number of early Americans had already started to lead a more settled kind of life.

There is, for example, a cave in Illinois called the Modoc Rock Shelter, which lies in a bluff overlooking the Mississippi River. The earliest inhabitants of the cave lived there more than 9,000 years ago, a time when big-game hunting still flourished on the Great Plains. Yet the bones and other rubbish that these people left on the floor of the cave show that they were not wandering hunters of bison and mammoths. They hunted local game: raccoons, opossums, deer, and elk. The bones of catfish and the shells of mussels, snails, and turtles show that they took much of their food from the river.

The earliest Modoc people depended mostly on a year-round

Excavating at the Modoc Rock Shelter near the Mississippi River.

At the Modoc Rock Shelter, nineteen feet below the surface, diggers gently remove dust and dirt from an ancient skeleton. Their tools include trowels, small brushes—and infinite patience.

supply of animal foods. But by 8,000 years ago they had broadened their diet. Milling and grinding stones show that they were eating seeds, nuts, and roots. They were also eating ducks and geese. They still hunted deer, but they did so with a light spear and a spear thrower. They used both bone and stone for making tools, and they made ornaments out of shells and stones.

This way of life, which is called Eastern Archaic, became increasingly widespread as big game became more and more scarce.

Changing Times, Changing Ways 49

For ornaments, tools, and other objects, the Modoc people used not only stone and bone but also shells from the Mississippi River.

Meanwhile, a somewhat different way of life had been established in the deserts of the Southwest. Also Archaic, it is called the Desert culture. The desert people hunted small game when they could and collected seeds, fruits, and roots. They used plant fibers to make footwear and baskets. Although this was a difficult way of life, it, too, became increasingly widespread. The changing climate had turned the Southwest and the Great Basin into harsh, dry lands, where people were forced to turn chiefly toward plants for their needs.

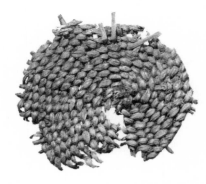

Objects made by people of the Desert culture. The curved object, about a foot long, is a wrench made from the horn of a bighorn sheep. It was used to straighten arrow or dart shafts.

The Archaic ways of life probably continued for a few thousand years, but they were bound to change, because the Archaic people lived in a wide variety of places and climates. As groups discovered the best local sources of food and the best ways of hunting, catching, or collecting it, they became specialists. By about 4,000 years ago a number of distinct cultures had arisen, and by 2,000 years ago some of these were highly developed.

For example, more than 4,000 years ago Indians living in what is now Boston developed fishing into a major industry. While modern workmen were digging the foundation for a building in the Back Bay section of Boston, they came upon a line of upright stakes. Further exploration showed that there was a two-acre area containing some 65,000 pointed wooden stakes. They had been driven into the mud and interlaced with brush to form a system of weirs for trapping fish in what was then a shallow lagoon.

In the same period other Indians of the East had learned to make pottery. And some had started to cultivate seeds and plants.

By 2,000 years ago a highly developed culture was flourishing among Indians of the Middle West. These Indians were hunters, collectors of shellfish, gatherers of food plants, and, latterly, farmers. They had a large population, which was organized into social classes and probably ruled by a central government. They are best known for the mounds in which they buried their dead. The earliest mounds were simple ones, but as the culture developed, the mounds became larger and more elaborate. Some of the later mounds and earthworks covered several square miles.

Buried along with the dead were rich and artistic grave goods. The grave goods show the skill of the craftsmen who made them. They also show that these people had developed trade and transportation, because the raw materials were imported from other regions: copper from the shores of Lake Superior, conch shells from the Gulf of Mexico, mica from the Appalachians, alligator

Above: A huge mound in the shape of a serpent, apparently eating an egg. Circled by a modern road, the mound is more than a quarter of a mile long. Below: A nineteenth-century painting entitled "Huge Mound and the Manner of Opening Them."

teeth from Florida, stone from Wisconsin and Minnesota. These materials were worked into delicate ornaments, knives, beading, stone statuettes, and tobacco pipes shaped like animals.

At about the same time, some Indians of the Southwest were building apartment houses with as many as 800 rooms. They were skilled at making baskets and pottery, at weaving, and at making household tools. They grew crops on land that they irrigated. They held religious ceremonies and had a rich artistic life.

A mother and child, living about 2,000 years ago in what is now Ohio, were carved in wood by an artist of the Mound Builders.

Remains of kivas—large rooms for religious ceremonies—at Pueblo Bonito in New Mexico's Chaco Canyon.

In the same general area, other Indians had built a tremendous irrigation system, drawing on the waters of the Gila and Salt rivers. They built dams on the rivers and dug canals to carry water away from the dams. Some of the canals were more than twenty-five miles long and as much as forty feet wide. These were people who borrowed many ideas from Middle America, and they built pyramids, made beautiful pottery and jewelry, and played court games with rubber balls.

Both of these great cultures of the Southwest were based on agriculture. Agriculture frees men from having to search for food by providing a local year-round supply. If enough crops are raised, they can feed a large number of people, and a large population requires the development of laws and government. If farming is efficient, it can be carried out by part of the population, freeing the rest to develop crafts, services, and professions. In short, agriculture can supply the roots of civilization.

Model of Pueblo Bonito. Here prehistoric Indians developed the largest apartment house built anywhere in the world before 1882.

The great civilizations of the Mayas, the Aztecs, and the Incas were based on agriculture, as were all the higher cultures of the New World. Of the many plants these people raised and ate, far and away the most important was corn. It was the key plant that allowed large-scale farming and large villages, for it has a high yield and it stores well.

Like modern corn, the corn these people grew had long rows of kernels, or seeds, which grew on cobs and were enveloped in husks. Then, as now, corn could exist only as a cultivated plant and could not grow wild. Unlike wheat or rye, corn cannot seed itself, because its seeds are wrapped in husks. If the cobs fall to the ground, the next year young plants will sprout so thickly that none can get enough moisture and nourishment; usually they all die out.

For many years those facts confronted scientists with a large problem. If there is no wild corn and if corn cannot grow wild, where did it come from in the first place?

The answer was finally discovered in 1960 by archeologists digging in caves of the Tehuacán Valley in Mexico. The earliest people who lived in these caves, about 12,000 years ago, were hunters of birds, rabbits, and other small animals and collectors of plants. As time passed, the people of the caves began to make greater use of plants. By 8,000 years ago they were growing some plants, such as squash. By 7,000 years ago they had discovered corn. It was then a tiny wild plant, capable of seeding itself, with ears the size of a thumbnail. With man's help, over thousands of years, this tiny wild plant became the corn on which New World agriculture depended and which existed in hundreds of varieties.

Prehistoric art objects found in Arizona, left to right: Picture of a frog etched about 1,000 years ago, perhaps with fermented cactus juice, on a shell from the Pacific coast; white stone mortar, carved to represent a bighorn sheep; a 3,000-year-old deer made of split twigs; 1,100-year-old bowl painted with dancing figures.

Maya sculpture of rain god.

By 5,000 years ago the Tehuacán cave people were raising about a third of the food they ate. By 3,500 years ago they had become villagers with social and religious organizations. By 2,000 years ago they were building irrigation canals, growing a wide variety of plants, including peanuts and tomatoes, and raising turkeys. They traded with other peoples. They practiced art, religion, and government. And they became in time a people called the Mixtec, who ruled the area until they were conquered by the Aztecs.

The finds at Tehuacán are of great importance. They have revealed the wild ancestor of domestic corn. They have shown how new ideas and methods develop out of older ones. And they have shown how a band of people who lived by gathering plants and hunting small animals evolved into a people who had a high civilization that was based on agriculture. These discoveries are evidence that earlier scholars were wrong in thinking that all great advances in the New World must have been introduced from the Old World. The caves at Tehuacán show New World people slowly discovering how to domesticate wild plants and how to raise them.

Nonetheless, there is some evidence that the Indians, the first settlers of the New World, did from time to time have contact with peoples from distant lands. The evidence is tantalizingly clouded by the mists of time. But a growing number of archeologists have come to believe that the New World was visited—both by accident and on purpose—by people from other lands hundreds and even thousands of years before Columbus made his first landfall in the Bahamas.

Visitors from Distant Lands?

Some time ago a rock with a Latin inscription was found on the coast of Maine. The lettering was much weathered, but it could still be read. Carved in the rock were a few lines from Virgil's epic poem the *Aeneid*.

To some people this worn carving was evidence that a Roman ship had been wrecked on the Maine coast. They imagined its hapless sailors creating a sign of their presence, as later shipwrecked sailors did with verses from the Bible.

But the carving is not evidence that any serious scholar can accept. It looks old, because it has been weathered, but there is no way of dating it. The lines are in Latin, but they are from a poem familiar to generations of students; there is no way of telling whether the inscription was carved by a shipwrecked Roman or by an American student of Latin. And so the rock tells us only that at some unknown time some unknown person carved a few lines of the *Aeneid* on it.

Another slab of carved stone, which was found in Brazil, raises the question of whether the Phoenicians reached the New World about 2,500 years ago. The Phoenicians, a Semitic people of the Mediterranean, were the most skilled and fearless navigators of the Ancient World. Their ships of trade plied the Mediterranean and sailed where others dared not go—through the Pillars of Hercules (the Strait of Gibraltar) and into the Atlantic. Following routes of their own discovery, the Phoenicians traded along the Atlantic coast of Europe, sailing as far north as Britain.

Around 600 B.C., according to the Greek historian Herodotus, Phoenicians became the first people to sail around the coast of Africa. Describing the voyage, Herodotus wrote that the Phoeni-

cians set out from the Gulf of Aqaba and sailed southward. Once a year they went ashore, sowed the land, and waited until the grain was ready to harvest. Then, having gathered in the crop, they sailed on. And so it came to pass that two whole years went by, and it was not until the third that they rounded the Pillars of Hercules, entered the Mediterranean, and came to Egypt.

Herodotus does not mention the loss of a ship. But a few modern scholars argue that one ship was blown off course in a storm, caught in a westward-flowing current off Africa, and carried across the Atlantic to Brazil. They base their argument on the slab of stone that was found in 1872 on a plantation at Parahyba in Brazil.

The stone was covered with strange carvings, later identified as Phoenician writing. Translated, the text told how Phoenician sailors had left the Gulf of Aqaba with ten ships, sailed through the Red Sea, and for two years traveled in convoy around Africa, until a storm separated one ship from the others. "So we have come here," the text read, "twelve men and three women on a new shore which I, the admiral, control."

Ever since the text was first published, scholars of ancient languages have argued heatedly about it. Some have thought it genuine. Others have thought it one more of the clever forgeries that scholarly practical jokers have created from time to time and left for other scholars to "discover" and argue about.

The root of the argument has to do with word use and grammar. Some scholars argue that the text cannot be a forgery, because it contains forms of grammar and word usage that have only recently been identified as Phoenician; therefore they could not have been known to a forger of 1872 or earlier. Other scholars, however, say that the text is an improbable hodgepodge of Phoenician and Hebrew and cannot be genuine.

Another problem is that scholars cannot study the stone itself.

They must work from copies of the text or copies of copies, which may not be accurate. The stone itself disappeared shortly after its discovery.

At present there is no way of being sure about the text from Parahyba. The Phoenicians were certainly one of the early peoples who could have crossed the Atlantic. They were expert sailors, with ocean-going ships twice the size of Columbus', and there is a westward-flowing current that would carry a ship from southern Africa to Brazil. But so far there is no reliable evidence that the Phoenicians reached Brazil or any other part of the New World.

Archeologists would be very pleased to find something like the Parahyba stone, provided they could prove it genuine. But in their search for signs of early contacts between the Old World and the New, they do not really expect to find "calling cards" carved in stone. They look instead for ideas and objects that suddenly appear in a culture and that seem to have come from nowhere within that culture.

Suppose, for example, that archeologists discover when a certain group of people began to make and use pottery. If the early pottery is clumsily made and experimental, this suggests that the people either invented the idea of pottery making or came upon

Phoenician writing, copied from the Parahyba stone.

the idea and developed a technique for making it. If, however, the early pottery is well made, this suggests that the people learned the art from others who had already developed it. If well-made pottery is very much like that already in use somewhere else, this points to a contact between the two groups.

Evidence of this kind has convinced many archeologists that the New World was visited a number of times by early voyagers from Asia. One such voyage may have taken place about 5,000 years ago, when some Japanese fishermen seem to have reached Ecuador.

What appears to be the earliest pottery so far discovered in the New World was dug out of the ground near the fishing village of Valdivia in Ecuador, and it dates from about 5,000 years ago. The people who lived there at the time were hunters and gatherers, who took a large part of their food from the sea. They had simple stone tools for cutting, chopping, and scraping. They used pebbles as sinkers for their fishing lines, and they sawed fishhooks out of shells. Mixed in with the remains of shells, fishbones, and simple tools, archeologists found broken pottery.

When the pieces of pottery were sorted and studied, they provided a major surprise. They were not early attempts at pottery making but the product of practiced hands. They were fragments of vessels, or containers, that had been shaped and decorated in various ways. Something else was even more surprising. The shapes and decorations were very much like those of the Jomon

*5,000-year-old pottery found
in Ecuador (left in each
pair) resembles pottery of
Jomon in Japan
(right in each pair).*

culture on Kyushu, the southernmost island of Japan.

Carbon-14 dating gave the shells an age of about 5,000 years, and so the same age was given to the tools and pottery that had been mixed in with them. Five thousand years ago the Jomon people were living in much the same simple way as the people of coastal Ecuador, taking a large part of their food from the sea and making tools out of stone, shell, and bone. But there was one important difference. The Jomon people were skilled pottery makers. Pottery making in Japan is at least 9,000 years old, and the Jomon shapes and decorations had developed out of earlier ones.

The archeologists who found the pottery think that there is only one way to explain it. They believe that a boatload of Jomon deep-sea fishermen were caught in a typhoon and blown far out to sea in a northeasterly direction. There their boat was trapped in strong eastward-flowing currents, and they could not make their way back to Japan.

Perhaps, like many of the island people of the Pacific today, these fishermen knew how to keep themselves alive at sea in a small boat and did not panic when they lost their way. Currents and winds would have carried the boat generally eastward in a path that becomes southeasterly along the coast of North America. Off Lower California, some currents bear off to the west, while others flow southward. Apparently the fishermen continued south and made their landfall in Ecuador.

This story is not easy to believe. It seems almost impossible that the fishermen could have drifted 8,000 miles and landed in Ecuador, where they taught the Indians to make pottery. Yet archeologists cannot find another way to explain the sudden appearance of this particular pottery in a region where there are no traces of earlier pottery.

About 2,000 years ago, Ecuador seems to have had another visit by voyagers from Asia. The evidence is a collection of pottery objects that were common in Asia but have not been found anywhere else in the New World. They were discovered by archeologists digging near the coast north of Valdivia.

Among these objects are pottery models of houses. The houses have saddle roofs; that is, the ridge of the roof is low at the center and rises to high eaves at the ends. This kind of house was common in Southeast Asia and in Indonesia, but not in the New World.

A number of pottery figurines were found. In each of these seated figures the legs are folded one above the other. This posture is the same as that of figurines from India. Also, unlike other figurines from Ecuador, a number of these figures have beards.

Two other kinds of object were pottery earplugs, shaped like golf tees, and pottery neck rests, or head rests. Similar earplugs existed in Japan as much as 4,000 years ago. Starting about 4,500 years ago, neck rests were widely used in Egypt, India, China, and other parts of the Old World.

These pottery objects found together in one part of Ecuador are nearly impossible to explain, unless they were introduced by people from Asia. They appear suddenly in Ecuador. They seem unrelated to New World pottery objects, but they are like objects that were widely used in the Old World.

A somewhat different reason for thinking that early voyagers crossed the Pacific comes from the work of plant geographers,

INDOCHINA

JAVA

ECUADOR

ECUADOR

ECUADOR

Above: *Seated figures and pottery house models from the Old World and the New.* Left: *Pottery neck rest from Ecuador, strongly resembling neck rests from the Old World.*

who study the origin, development, and spread of plants.

One of the plants they have studied is the sweet potato. As far as anyone knows, the sweet potato originated in the New World. Like corn, it began as a wild plant that changed as it was cultivated by man until it could no longer reproduce itself without man's help. The sweet potato, a root, is grown by cutting shoots from its vine and planting them. It is not a plant that can be spread by wind or birds; nor can it drift across the ocean. Yet this New World plant was being grown in Polynesia, New Zealand, and Southeast Asia long before Europeans arrived.

There are many other cases of plants that seem to have had human help in spreading to or from the New World. There are also many scientific arguments about these plants, for the origins of cultivated plants are often difficult to trace. Nonetheless, the work of plant geographers supports the idea that a number of peoples could and did cross the Pacific.

This Ecuador raft strongly resembles the raft of a kind long used in Formosa (facing page).

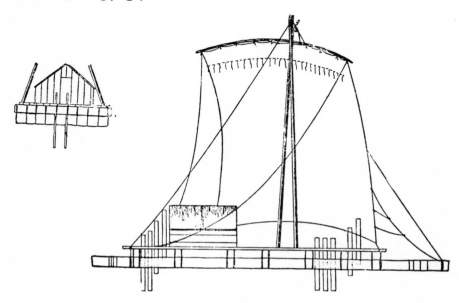

To people at home on the water, the sea is not so much a barrier as a highway, and the coastal people of Ecuador and northern Peru were at home on it. Several thousand years ago they were deep-sea fishermen; archeologists exploring layers of ancient rubbish have found the bones of deep-sea fish. Some 2,000 to 2,500 years ago people from northern Ecuador were active traders. Their goods are found up and down the coast of Ecuador, which probably means that the traders traveled by sea. Figures and pottery masks of Mexican style have been found on the coast of Ecuador but not in any land area between Mexico and Ecuador. These objects suggest a cultural contact that was carried on by sea.

The craft used in Ecuador were very likely the same kind of sea-going rafts that the Spaniards later saw. These were large sailing rafts of balsa logs that were equipped with movable centerboards and that were extremely seaworthy. They were also of a very complex design.

Both rafts are steered, not by a rudder or by oars, but by raising and lowering six to nine movable boards.

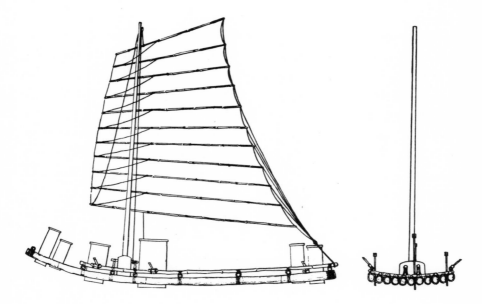

The origin of these rafts is one of many unsolved puzzles. Similar rafts have been used in Asia for at least 2,500 years, but no one knows whether the rafts were independently invented on opposite sides of the Pacific.

Unlike pottery neck rests, rafts would be a natural invention for a coastal people. But would two different peoples invent the same complex raft? It seems unlikely, and yet such things have happened.

In fairly modern times, for example, an astonishing number of inventions and discoveries have been made at the same time by different people. The invention of photography, the telescope, and the telephone and the discovery of the planet Neptune are four examples out of a very long list. In each case the invention or discovery was made by two or more men within a single year.

The origins of ancient inventions are, of course, much harder to find. Even so, it is possible that many useful ideas and objects were invented by one group of people and then independently invented again by another. Agriculture, for instance, appears to have been an Old World invention and also a New World invention.

On the other hand, it is almost impossible to believe that Asians and Mexican Indians independently invented the game of parcheesi and worked out the same set of complicated rules for playing it. (The board game we play is a very simple version of this ancient game.) It is much more likely that Old World visitors brought parcheesi to the New World.

A large number of other inventions, however, are of less clear-cut origin. So far, there is no way of being certain whether they spread from one people to another or were independently invented by two or more peoples.

The blowgun is one of these puzzling objects. A blowgun consists of a hollow tube of bamboo, fitted with a light dart that is tipped with strong poison. It is an accurate, silent weapon and ideal for hunting in forests, where the air is still and the dart will not be blown off course.

The blowgun is found only in the Amazon forests of South America and in the forests of Malaysia and Borneo. Most scholars think that the blowgun was independently invented in both places, because people living under the same conditions are likely to arrive at the same way of doing things. But a few scholars are less sure. They think the blowgun may well have crossed the Pacific and that it cannot be called an independent invention until we know more about its history.

The invention of the wheel is an even more puzzling question. The wheel is one of the great inventions of mankind, yet it was not used by Indians of the New World. Scholars long argued that the absence of the wheel in the New World proved two things. One was that the Indians had not invented the wheel. The other was that they could have had little or no contact with the Old World, or else they would have learned about the wheel. Then, in 1944, archeologists digging near Tampico, Mexico, came upon some small pottery animals that were mounted on wheels.

INDIA

MEXICO

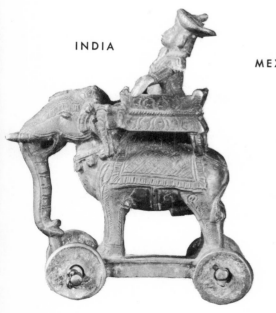

Animals on wheels. Did the Aztecs know about the wheel used in the Old World? Or did they invent it independently in the New World?

As these pottery animals showed, the Indians of Mexico had known about the wheel. Yet they had not put it to use and built wheeled vehicles. The main reason is probably that they lacked horses, donkeys, oxen, and other beasts of burden that could be trained to pull wheeled vehicles. Even so, the question remains: Did the Indians invent the wheel? Some scholars think they did but never put it to use. Others think they didn't, arguing that people do not make unnecessary inventions. These scholars think that the wheeled animals were introduced from Asia, where they were widely used in various religious cults.

These same scholars have found striking resemblances between the art of Middle America and the Hindu-Buddhist art of India and Southeast Asia. If there were no contacts between Asians and Middle Americans, then it is hard to explain why the art of both should use the same motifs: Atlas-like figures bearing heavy objects on their shoulders, tiger thrones, lotus staffs, seated lions, diving gods, and gods standing on crouched human figures. Both Hindu-Buddhist art and Maya art have the unusual custom of showing the rootlike stalk of the lotus, a part that grows under water or buried in mud. In both the lotus is used as a kind of imaginary landscape with human figures in it.

Sea-going rafts and blowguns could either have spread or have been independent inventions. The art motifs, like the pottery finds, are difficult to account for unless they were brought into the Americas. A number of scholars think that they were brought on Asian ships that crossed the Pacific on purpose and later returned home.

There are no reliable records of such voyages in Chinese literature, although there are fables and legends about unknown distant lands visited by Buddhist priests and other travelers. As with all such tales, it is hard to tell what is fact and what is fancy, and so there is no way of identifying the lands.

There are, however, reliable records having to do with Asian trade and colonies. These make clear that by at least 2,000 years ago Asian ships and navigators were capable of ocean-going voyages. By the third century A.D. both China and India had colonies in other parts of Asia. Political and trade links were maintained by sea through the use of ships capable of carrying 600 men and well over 1,000 tons of cargo.

A travel journal kept by a Chinese Buddhist tells of his return from India. He first sailed to Ceylon, where, his journal says, he took passage on a large merchant ship that carried more than 200 sailors and passengers. During a heavy gale, the ship was damaged and drifted helplessly for ninety days, eventually reaching Java. There the Buddhist took passage on another ship of the same size, which set out on a fifty-day run through the South China Sea to Canton. Beset by storms, the ship took eighty-two days to make the trip.

Both of these were large ships on regular runs, and they were well provisioned: they could feed some 200 people for three months. There is little doubt that such ships were capable of crossing the Pacific. Perhaps the first crossings were made by accident. Of the many Asian ships engaged in long sea voyages, some must have been caught in storms and carried far off course. If they were trapped in the currents that flow northeast, they would have been carried across the Pacific. (In much more recent times, winds and currents have driven disabled Japanese junks onto the Pacific shores of the New World. Glass floats from Japanese fishing nets are often found on these same shores.)

The sailors on such ships might well have managed to find their way home again. Currents would have carried them southward along the west coast of the Americas to a landfall in Mexico or in Ecuador. Off Middle America there is a westward-flowing current that would carry a ship to Indonesia. Another current off the

Borrowed from the Old World
— or —
Invented in the New World?

Stone club heads

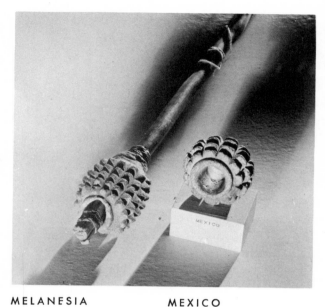

MELANESIA   MEXICO

Pan pipes

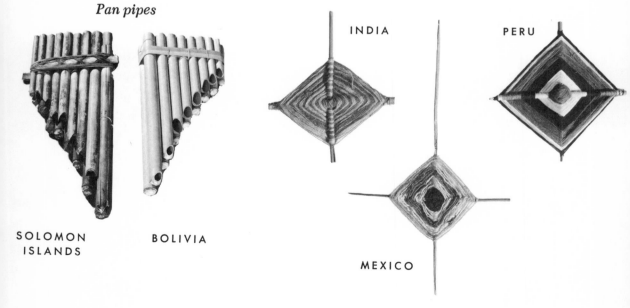

INDIA   PERU

SOLOMON
ISLANDS   BOLIVIA

MEXICO

String crosses

CAMBODIA

Sculpture motifs

MEXICO

EASTER ISLAND

CALIFORNIA

Stone fishhooks

coast of northern Peru and Ecuador flows toward Polynesia and the islands beyond. That is, there is a natural highway in the sea from Asia to the Americas and two such routes from the Americas to Asia.

A voyage across the Pacific is long, some 7,000 or 8,000 miles. But if a ship is traveling with a current, the distance to be sailed becomes much shorter, because the surface water is moving. Suppose a ship can make 60 miles a day under sail. If it is traveling in a current with an average speed of 40 miles a day, it will make 100 miles in a day. The effect is like that of walking up a rising escalator.

Then, too, it was a common practice among peoples of the Ancient World to follow the coastline instead of navigating across open bodies of water. It is possible to take just such a route from Asia to the New World—northeast past Japan, the Kurile Islands, and the Kamchatka Peninsula, eastward past the Aleutians, and then south along the west coast of the Americas. The route sounds roundabout, but it is not. Because the earth is a sphere, this route is no longer than sailing across the Pacific at the equator.

A ship following this route would be within sight and reach of land for large parts of the voyage. There would be landmarks, and there would be places to put in for food and water.

Such voyages would leave few traces along the way. If they took place, the evidence of them is most likely to be found at their destinations. It will be found in ideas and objects that seem to have no roots in New World cultures but that are rooted in the Old World. So far there is no reason to think that such contacts played an important part in the development of New World cultures. But there is still much to be learned about the origins of New World writing, mathematics, and working of metals.

If, as many archeologists now believe, Asians did make a number of voyages to the New World, they apparently stopped doing

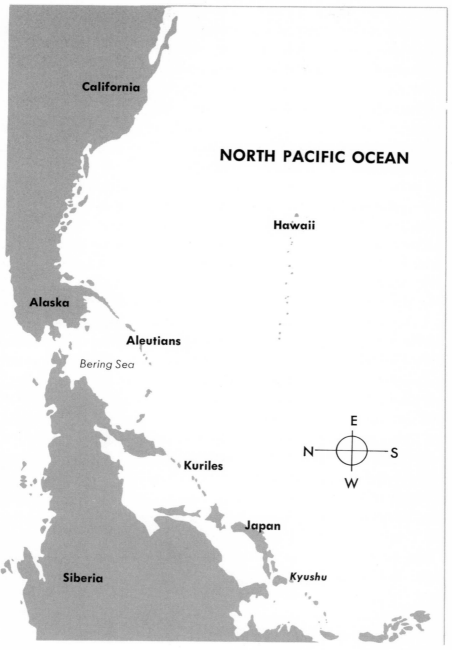

California

NORTH PACIFIC OCEAN

Hawaii

Alaska

Aleutians

Bering Sea

Kuriles

Japan

Siberia

Kyushu

E

N ◯ S

W

The modern way of drawing a map, with north at the top, is often misleading. This map, with east at the top, shows the North Pacific as Asians thought of it. The coastal route from the Old World to the New is almost a straight line.

so after a while. Perhaps the voyages were made for trade but did not prove worthwhile. Some scholars have suggested that persecution at home caused Buddhists to set out in search of a new home. Perhaps that need ceased to exist.

Where there is no written history, it is difficult to look backward through time. It is like trying to study a landscape that is screened by mist. Certain large shapes stand out. Here or there the mist lifts for a moment, revealing a fence post or a cow. But it is difficult even to imagine what the whole scene looks like. In the same way, archeologists and other students of the past find that the mists of time obscure their view. Did Japanese fishermen and visitors from a Hindu-Buddhist culture once mingle with the Indians of Middle and South America? Or are those blurred shapes really something else?

In addition, there are a few other shapes that are even harder to make out, for here the clues are not things that a scholar can handle and photograph, such as pottery, but legends and myths. They deal with bearded, fair-skinned gods who lived among the Indians from Brazil to Peru to Mexico, taught them many things, and then sailed away across the ocean.

When the Spaniards set about their conquest of the Aztecs and the Incas, they were greatly aided by these legends. Seeing the white skins and the beards of these strangers, the Indians at first thought that the fair-skinned gods had returned. The Aztec leader waited too long to defend his empire against Cortés. In Peru, Francisco Pizarro with a handful of men was able to capture the Sun-King and his huge empire without a fight.

The legends lived on among the Indians, who told the Spaniards of the many wondrous things the fair-skinned gods had taught them and done.

Legends alone prove nothing, for they can as well be based on fancy as on fact. Yet a few curious observations suggest that there may be some truth in these legends. When the Spaniards discovered the Inca Empire, they noted that most of the Indians were small and dark. But members of the ruling family were tall and more fair-skinned than the Spaniards; some had red hair. In the desert sands near the Pacific coast, mummies have been found in burial caves. Some resemble present-day Indians and have stiff black hair. Others have long skulls, tall bodies, and silky chestnut or red hair.

Who are they? No one knows. But the legend, the Spanish observations, and the mummies suggest the possibility that northern Europeans reached South America in the period when they were crossing the North Atlantic to Greenland and Vinland.

Painting by an Aztec artist. At the left, an armed and mounted Spaniard receives a friendly welcome. But, at the right, a Spaniard kills Aztecs near one of their temples.

In Greenland, archeologists study the remains of a Norse settlement.

Who Discovered America?

Vinland the Good

Toward the end of the eighth century A.D., at a time when much of Europe was under the rule of Charlemagne, Viking seafarers began a series of raids from the north. The raids marked the start of the Viking Era: a span of some 250 years when a tremendous outpouring of energy carried men of the north to such far-flung places as Greenland and Bagdad.

The Vikings were Scandinavians, men of Norway, Denmark, and Sweden. Today the name is used to mean all the Norsemen of the Viking Era, but at the time, "Viking" meant a pirate or raider from the north. To their own people Vikings were the men whose swift ships carried them over the seas for lightning raids on foreign coasts. Armed with shields, double-edged swords, and battle-axes, the bearded Viking raiders swarmed ashore, killing, plundering, and carrying off slaves in attacks that were known and feared from the British Isles to North Africa.

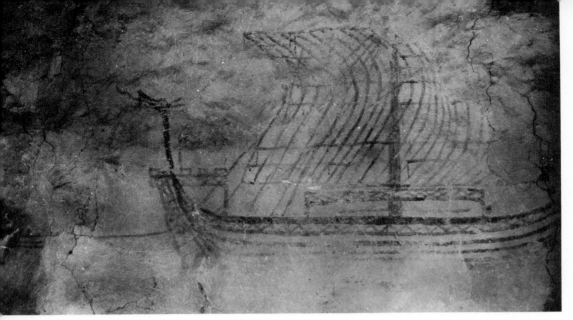

Norse ship under full sail, as drawn centuries ago on a church wall in Norway, shows a later version of the Viking ship. The development of large, swift sailing vessels—much more seaworthy than others of the time—made possible the rapid expansion of Viking trade, piracy, and exploration.

During this same period, however, many other Northmen sailed forth from their homelands not as raiders but as traders and settlers. During the Viking Era these people colonized parts of England and France and all of Sicily. They established the first Russian kingdom. They traded slaves and furs for Chinese silks and Arab silver in the markets of Bagdad. And before this great explosion of trade and travel ended, they settled Iceland, founded colonies in Greenland, and discovered the land that they called Vinland the Good.

Most of our information about the westward movement across the Atlantic comes from the sagas. These stories of great Viking adventures were passed on from generation to generation until, in the twelfth century, they began to be written down.

Sagas tell us that the Viking discovery of Iceland was made by accident soon after A.D. 860. The discoverers were Viking sailors who were blown far off course by storms and so came to Iceland. A few years later, two foster brothers, Leif and Ingolf, began the settlement of Iceland. Leif had been outlawed from Norway for

Elaborately carved stern of a Viking ship unearthed at Oseberg in Norway in 1904. It was the burial ship for a high-born woman of the ninth century, very likely Queen Asa. The ship contained all the belongings she might need in an afterlife.

The North Atlantic as it appeared to the Scandinavians. On this map, west is at the top. From the mountains of Greenland, on a clear day, the Viking settlers could see land to the westward.

causing a quarrel in which two young nobles were killed. He and his brother sailed to Iceland, liked what they saw, and decided to move there. Ingolf went back to Norway to arrange the move, while Leif made a quick raid on Ireland, plundering and taking slaves to help with the settlement. With their families, slaves, cattle, household goods, and loot, the brothers set out for Iceland in 874 and became its first Norse settlers.

Other colonists soon arrived. By the year 930, between 20,000 and 30,000 people had settled homesteads in the area around present-day Reykjavik. The land did not lend itself to farming, but there was good pasturage on which the settlers raised sheep and cattle. Fishing was excellent. There were birds to hunt and eggs to collect. There were seals in the harbors, and sometimes a stranded whale provided meat. Trade was carried on with Norway, Ireland, and England.

Historians do not agree on what caused the large movements of people to Iceland. But the most likely explanation is that Iceland was settled by men who came to seek land, which was scarce in Scandinavia, and the freedom of their own rule. Whatever the cause, only sixty years after the arrival of the first settlers, there was no more habitable land to be had in Iceland, and in 975 the first great famine occurred. It is not surprising that there were people ready to move on when the time came, as it soon did.

In 982 Eric the Red was banished from Iceland for three years because of his part in an outbreak of killings. He decided to investigate a land to the west that had been sighted earlier but never explored. Eric took his ship and crew to the barren, glacier-edged coast of eastern Greenland, sailed around the southern tip, and turned up the west coast. Here the land looked promising. The coast was fringed with fjords (long, narrow inlets) and green with grassy slopes. Best of all, there were no people. The land was his for the taking.

Ruins of a Norse church in Greenland.

Eric spent three years exploring the new land. Apart from two good green strips on the western coast, most of it was covered by a huge icecap. He found, however, that the land was rich in game and the sea was full of fish, seals, and walruses. Summers on the west coast were short but pleasant, and the pastures were sheltered by low hills. When his years of exile were up, Eric returned to Iceland with news of this land, to which he gave the attractive name of Greenland, and began to gather settlers.

When Eric sailed again for Greenland in 986, he led a fleet of at least twenty-five ships, carrying colonists, livestock, and household goods. Fourteen of the ships arrived safely, the rest having either turned back or been lost at sea, and the first colony of perhaps 450 settlers was established. It soon grew to between 2,000 and 3,000 people, the most these two green strips could support.

It was from Greenland that the next voyages westward took place. The story of them is told in two different sagas. One is called *The Greenlanders' Saga*. The other is *The Saga of Eric the Red*, which is also called *The Karlsefni Saga*.

Wooden cross with runes from the Greenland church mentioned in The Saga of Eric the Red. *Although the Vikings used runes to carve brief inscriptions on wood, metal, or rock, they did not use runes for ordinary writing. To record laws, events, or family history, the Vikings relied on memory and oral tradition.*

In *The Greenlanders' Saga*, the first sighting of land west of Greenland is credited to an Icelander named Bjarni Herjolfsson. Bjarni was a shipowner engaged in trade between Norway and Iceland. In the summer of 986 he sailed for Iceland, intending to spend the winter with his father there. On arriving he learned that his father had sold the homestead and moved to Greenland with Eric. Bjarni set out to follow his father. The sea ahead was unknown to him, but he was sure that he would recognize the fjords and snow-covered mountains of Greenland when he saw them.

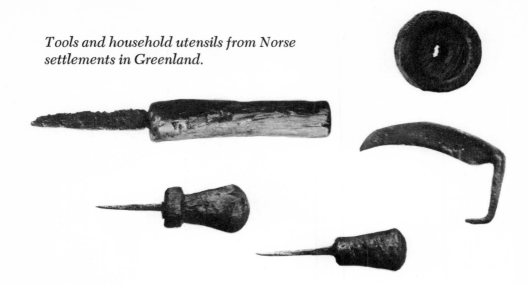

Tools and household utensils from Norse settlements in Greenland.

Three days out of Iceland, the ship was driven south by winds and then ran into fog. For days the ship drifted through the fog and Bjarni and his crew had no idea of which way they were going. Then the sun broke through, and they spread their sails and took fresh bearings. Soon they sighted a land of forests and low hills. Whatever this was, Bjarni knew it was not Greenland. So he turned north and sailed along the coast for two days. The land flattened out, although the forests continued. Another three days' sailing brought them to a high land that was covered with mountains and glaciers. To Bjarni this land looked unlike Greenland and good for nothing, and so he sailed on to the east. In four days' time he came to Greenland, where he settled with his father and gave up his voyaging.

Intent on reaching Greenland, Bjarni had not stopped to explore the lands he had sighted. And, since the Greenlanders were busy settling one new land, it was fifteen years before anyone set out to explore the other lands to the west. The person who did was Leif Ericsson, son of Eric the Red.

Leif bought Bjarni's ship and gathered a crew. He had expected his father to take charge of the voyage, but as Eric was riding down to the ship, he fell off his horse and was injured. So the ship sailed under the command of Leif.

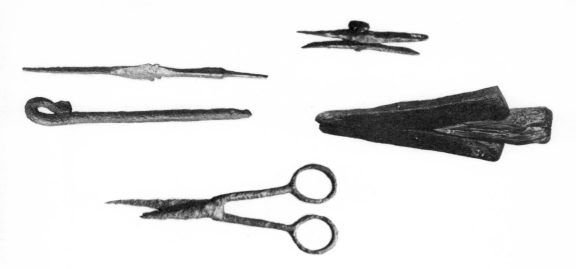

Sailing Bjarni's course in reverse, Leif came first to Bjarni's third landfall, a barren land with not even a blade of grass. Inland the ground was covered with great glaciers. Between the glaciers and the sea, the land was like one flat rock. Leif named the place Helluland, meaning Flatstone Land, and sailed on.

The second land Leif and his men came to was low-lying and wooded, with wide beaches of white sand that sloped gently into the sea. Leif named this place Markland, meaning Woodland, and again sailed on.

Two days later they sighted a third land. They first went ashore on an island, where they found grass sweet with dew. Then they sailed between the island and a cape that reached northward from the mainland, took the ship up a river, and anchored. They unloaded and built booths—shelters made of boughs.

Leif soon decided to build houses here and spend the winter, for this was fine country where salmon, game, and grass were plentiful and where the climate seemed so mild that the cattle they had brought should be able to graze the grass all winter. He also sent out scouting parties to explore the land. One evening a German member of the crew came back very late in a state of great excitement and reported that he had found grapevines and grapes, something he knew well, since they grew in his homeland.

Vinland the Good   87

When Leif sailed for Greenland, he took a cargo of timber, grape-vines, and grapes, having given the name Vinland to the place where he and his men had wintered.

On their return to Greenland, they found that Eric had died during the winter. Leif, as Eric's oldest son, took over the responsibilities of the colony, and so he gave the use of his ship to his brother Thorvald, who proposed to explore a much larger area than Leif had. Thorvald and his men reached Vinland without difficulty and spent the winter at Leif's camp, Leifsbudir (Leif's Booths). In spring and summer some of the men explored to the west, where they found beautiful country of woods, beaches, and islands. They saw no sign of people, except for a wooden building on an island, which was used for storing grain.

The second summer Thorvald and his crew sailed east and north, where they found a forested headland so beautiful that Thorvald thought he would like to build his homestead there. When they went ashore, they saw three mounds, which turned out to be three skin boats. Under each of the boats were three Skraelings, a name the Norsemen used for both Eskimos and Indians. Thorvald and his men set upon the Skraelings and killed them all, except for one who escaped in a boat. By morning the Greenlanders found themselves under attack from countless Skraelings in skin boats. During the fight Thorvald was fatally wounded by an arrow. He asked his men to bury him on the headland where he had wished to live. When they had done this, the men sailed back to Leifsbudir, where they spent the winter and took on a cargo of grapes and vines before returning to Greenland.

The next voyage was attempted by Eric's third son, Thorstein, who set out with his wife Gudrid in the same ship to bring back Thorvald's body. But Thorstein never reached Vinland. The ship was tossed about at sea all summer, finally returning to Greenland, where Thorstein fell ill and died of a winter sickness.

Beautifully made Viking weapons, found in Scandinavia.

So far the Greenlanders had not tried to start a colony in Vinland, but the next voyager did. He was an Icelander named Thorfinn Karlsefni, who had sailed to Greenland with a cargo, stayed on, and married Thorstein's widow, Gudrid. Karlsefni and Gudrid set out with a party of sixty men, five women, and all kinds of livestock. They landed at Leifsbudir, where the men spent much of their time cutting and dressing timber.

In summer Skraelings appeared out of the woods, carrying bundles of furs. They wished to trade the furs for weapons, but Karlsefni forbade this and instead traded milk for the furs. Early in the second winter the Skraelings returned, again bringing furs for trade, but this time one of the Skraelings tried to steal some weapons. A fight broke out and a number of Skraelings were killed. Karlsefni decided that the dangers of Vinland were too great for a small colony. The following spring he loaded his ship with furs, timber, vines, and grapes and took his party back to Greenland.

The final voyage in this saga was organized by Freydis, Eric's daughter and a cruel and treacherous woman. She persuaded two Icelanders, brothers who had recently arrived in Greenland, to join her expedition with their ship in return for a half share in the

Viking carriage, elaborately carved, found in the Oseberg burial ship shown on page 81. Fifteen horses were buried with the ship, as well as four dogs and a sleigh.

profits. Once arrived in Vinland, Freydis took over Leifsbudir and forced the Icelanders to make camp elsewhere. Later, Freydis arranged the murder of everyone in the Icelanders' camp, added the cargo they had collected to her own, and returned to Greenland.

The dates of the voyages in this saga are not clear, but they seem to have started around the year 1000 and to have ended by 1020. *The Greenlanders' Saga* ends by telling of the good life that Karlsefni and Gudrid later lived in Iceland. Before they settled there, however, they sailed from Greenland to Norway to sell their cargo. While they were in Norway, they were visited by a man from the German town of Bremen, who admired the figure-

Head of a Viking, a decorative carving on the Oseberg carriage.

head of their ship and bought it from them. It had been carved of a wood called *mösurr* from Vinland.

The Saga of Eric the Red, or *The Karlsefni Saga,* is a shorter story that does not mention Bjarni's voyage but makes Leif the accidental, storm-blown discoverer of Vinland. It is chiefly concerned with Karlsefni's voyage, in which Thorvald and Freydis also take part. That is, three voyages from *The Greenlanders' Saga* appear here as one.

According to this saga, Karlsefni set out for Vinland with three ships and 160 men, following a route that took them to Helluland and Markland and past beaches of remarkable length. In this saga, however, two settlements are mentioned. One was in a fjord, which they named Straumfjord (Current Fjord), where the land was beautiful and mountainous, the hunting and fishing good, and the winter bitterly cold. The other settlement was farther south and named Hóp, which means a landlocked bay. Hóp was a pleasant place of tall trees and wild grapes, where no snow fell in winter. Here Skraelings arrived, trading furs for pieces of red cloth. The first encounter between the Skraelings and the settlers was peaceful, but the second was not. And so Karlsefni decided that the time had come to leave.

In spite of their differences, both sagas tell of voyages to lands west of Greenland. Both tell of Vinland the Good, where trees grow tall and grapes grow wild and cattle can feed on grass all winter. Therefore, if the sagas are telling of real events, this pleasant land can only have been part of North America.

Do the sagas tell of real events? Scholars have long argued the question. The stories were told and retold for 200 years before being written down. Were they true or invented to begin with? Did the stories change and grow in the telling? Were they written down just as they were told? For a long time, no one could be sure. Today, however, most scholars think that the basic events of these sagas are true, and they think so for several reasons.

One has to do with people who lack a written history. The only way they can keep their history—and so know their past and their forefathers—is to tell the events as they occurred. That is, there is an obligation to tell truly what has been. This is so today of peoples who do not write, and there is every reason to think that it was so of the Northmen, too.

The Vikings of Scandinavia accumulated treasure from trade, from piracy—and from their own expert craftsmen. Archeologists have found many buried collections of coins and silver ornaments, like the ones shown here.

A second reason is that the discovery of Vinland was known to a number of people outside Greenland. Vinland is mentioned, for example, in a sort of world geography written by Adam of Bremen and finished around 1075. Adam had spent some time with Svein, king of the Danes, collecting information about the northern seas. From Svein he learned of a place called Vinland, which had been discovered in the ocean and visited a number of times and which was famous for its wild grapes. Another early writer who mentioned Vinland was Ari Thorgilsson, who was the first Icelandic

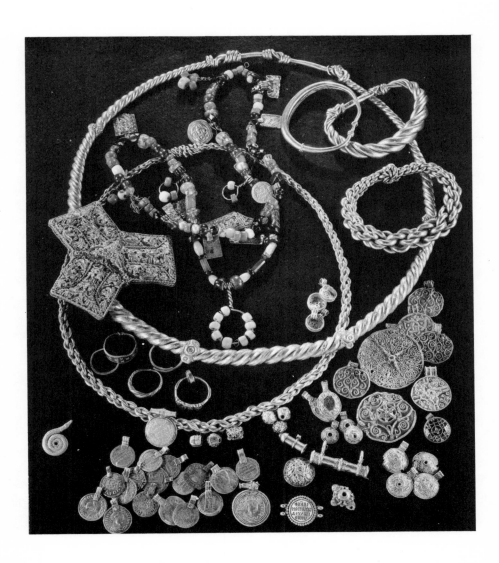

historian and whose grandfather had been a cousin of Thorfinn Karlsefni's. In his *Book of Icelanders,* which he finished about 1121, Ari did not describe Vinland but simply referred to it as if it were a place that everyone knew about and that needed no explanation.

Another piece of evidence, which may prove very important, is the Vinland map. Discovered in Europe in 1957, it is a map of the world that shows two large islands west of Iceland. One is clearly Greenland, and to the west of it is an even larger island. A Latin inscription identifies the second island as "Island of Vinland, discovered by Bjarni and Leif in company." Some scholars think that the map is a clever twentieth-century forgery. Others think it is genuine and was copied in the middle 1400's from an earlier map. If it is genuine, the map proves the discovery of Vinland by Northmen beyond doubt, for no one outside the northern countries had the knowledge to draw such an accurate map of Greenland.

Another reason for believing the sagas is that the findings of archeologists tend to support them. For example, the sagas tell us that Eric the Red remained a pagan all his life, faithful to the old gods and the old ways. But his son Leif became a convert to Christianity while on a visit to Norway and returned to spread the faith in Greenland. One of Leif's converts was his mother, who built the first Christian church in Greenland. Not long ago archeologists discovered the remains of the church built by Leif's mother at Brattahlid, a few hundred yards from the foundations of Leif's house.

For these and still other reasons, most scholars today accept the voyages to Vinland as fact. They agree that Vinland must have been on the eastern coast of North America, but beyond that there is little agreement. The big question facing archeologists and historians is: Where was Vinland?

The Vinland map, if authentic, shows that the Greenlanders not only had sailed around all of their huge icy homeland but also had explored a large area of the North American coast.

The Clues to Vinland

Somewhere on the eastern coast of North America there is a pleasant region with fertile soil that was once known as Vinland the Good. The problem is to identify it, for Norse visits to Vinland were made by handfuls of people who stayed only a brief time, and the traces of them must be few and faint. Unlike Europe, Vinland can have no buried hoards of Viking plunder or burial ships for kings and queens. Unlike Greenland, Vinland can have no outlines of settlements marked by the foundations of 300 houses and their outbuildings. At most, Vinland might yield a few foundations, some tools or weapons, a grave, or a stone with a few words carved in the Vikings' ancient runes.

The area in which such scanty evidence may lie is huge. Vinland could be anywhere from northern Newfoundland to Chesapeake Bay. That is one of the few things on which scholars who study the sagas agree.

Over the years, the sagas have been the chief source of clues in the search for Vinland. Scholars have tried to match landmarks and anchorages of the sagas with present-day places along the coast. They have tried to match the Skraelings with particular groups of Eskimos or Indians. Most of all, they have tried to find a place that matched the description of Vinland. None of this is easy, because the clues in the sagas can be read in many ways.

For example, Vinland is described as a land of mild climate where no snow fell and cattle could graze in the open all winter. Does that mean it was a southerly land? At first glance, the answer seems to be yes, but it could equally well be no. The men who explored Vinland were used to the winters of Greenland, Iceland, and Scandinavia. Compared with these, a New England or Newfoundland winter might seem mild indeed. It is also true that livestock from Greenland were as hardy and used to cold as their owners. Read that way, the sagas may simply be saying that Vinland's winter was milder than Greenland's. They do say that no snow fell, and they may mean just that. Or they may mean that compared with Greenland, little snow fell. Or the lack of snow may be an element that crept into the sagas, as tellers emphasized the mildness of climate.

Vinland is described as a land where wild grapes grew. At the present time wild grapes grow along the coast only as far north as Portland, Maine. Does that mean Vinland must have been south of Maine? Some scholars would say yes. Others say no, and their reason has to do with the meaning of "Vinland."

They point out that *vin* is a very old Norse word that originally meant "pasture" or "grass." They think that Vinland was named for its grassy pastures and that there were no grapes. Later on, when writers such as Adam of Bremen heard about Vinland, they gave *vin* its newer meaning of "grapes" or "wine." They thought that because the new land was named Wineland, it must have grapes, and so they added grapes and grapevines to the story.

Other scholars, however, do not accept this idea. They say that *vin* had ceased to mean "pasture" long before the discovery of Vinland. They also think that the grapes are too important to be an invention and that Vinland was indeed a land of wild grapes. If they are right, then Vinland must have been at least as far south as New England.

There are many other examples of the different ways that the clues can be read, and there are probably almost as many opinions about Vinland as there are scholars studying this subject. Nonetheless, a number of archeologists and historians have come to think that Vinland was at least partly a northern land. They think that the forbidding land of mountains, glaciers, and flat stone named Helluland can only have been the southern part of Baffin Island. If so, then the second land, named Markland for its woods, must have been Labrador. And the third land, Vinland, was Newfoundland.

To us Newfoundland does not seem much like Vinland the Good, for it is a chilly, rather barren island, where no grapes grow. To Greenlanders, however, it may have looked very different. They were not farmers looking for farmland, but hunters, fishermen, and keepers of livestock looking for a place to continue this way of life. They were also men from a treeless arctic land. To them Newfoundland may have seemed good beyond their dreams. The land abounded with game and the waters with fish. There was good pasture on the northern coast. There were great forests of spruce, balsam fir, and birch. The climate was comparatively mild. And the earth held something else they needed—iron ore for making tools and weapons.

Another reason for thinking that Newfoundland was Vinland is its geographical position. An explorer from Greenland, following the Labrador coast southward, would have to come to Newfound-

A modern shed protects the remains of a Viking house built almost 1,000 years ago in Newfoundland. It had five rooms and a great hall.

land. And Newfoundland forces a choice on the explorer. He must either turn east and sail along the island's Atlantic coast or turn west and sail through the narrow strait that separates the northern tip of Newfoundland from the mainland.

A turning point is a likely place for explorers to go ashore. Since Newfoundland was the most attractive place the Greenlanders could have seen up to then, they may well have decided to build a base there and to explore other areas from it. A base on the tip of Newfoundland would have the added advantage of being easy to find again on later voyages—and in *The Greenlanders' Saga* Thorvald, Karlsefni, and Freydis were all able to find Leifs-budir without difficulty.

It was just such reasoning that led a Norwegian explorer and his archeologist wife to a major discovery. Thinking that the tip of Newfoundland was a logical place for Leif to have made his camp, they began a search and came upon the ruins of an early settlement near the tiny fishing village of L'Anse au Meadow.

The Clues to Vinland 99

Digging revealed traces of houses and of a smithy, where bog iron was processed into metal.

The remains of the houses are no more than beaten earth floors, the outlines of turf walls, and hearths. But the houses were built in the Norse style, also used in Greenland, and one had a great hall, in the Viking manner. Since the Indians and Eskimos did not build houses of this kind and did not know how to forge iron, there is no doubt that the settlement was built by outsiders.

Who were the outsiders? Besides the houses and smithy, only a few clues have been found. There are some very rusty nails and

Dr. Helge Ingstad, the Norwegian explorer who led the archeological expeditions to L'Anse au Meadow, at the Viking fireplace in the great hall.

Spindle whorl found at L'Anse au Meadow by Dr. Ingstad's wife, an archeologist. Before the day of the spinning wheel a spindle whorl, placed on a round shaft, was used to rotate the shaft while thread was being spun on it.

some fragments of iron, but the acidity of the soil has probably destroyed other clues of iron. Archeologists have also found a small piece of smelted copper, a stone lamp of the kind that was used in Iceland, a whetstone for needles, and a piece of bone needle. The most significant find to date is a soapstone spindle whorl, exactly like the whorls used in Norway in the early part of the eleventh century by women spinning wool. The discovery of the whorl suggests that there were women in the settlement. And since there is no soapstone near L'Anse au Meadow, the whorl must have been brought in, either from Norway or from Greenland, where there were many Norwegian goods.

The style of the houses, the spindle whorl, and other clues have convinced archeologists that the settlement was Norse. Carbon-14 dating of charcoal from the forge also points to a Norse settlement. The charcoal came from wood in trees that died between the years 860 and 1060. (Carbon-14 dating does not pinpoint a date but indicates a span of time.)

So far there is no way of telling exactly who these Norsemen were. But there is a chance that the little settlement was once known as Leifsbudir.

The location of the settlement suggests that this was the base from which the Greenlanders made voyages of exploration. Some of these voyages were to the south. So it is possible that Vinland became the name not just for one place but for a region that started in Newfoundland and reached south into New England. If so, many problems would be solved.

Grapes grow wild in New England. In the hardwood forests of southern New England, the Greenlanders would have found large numbers of grapevines. The same hardwood forests might have supplied the *mösurr* wood that both sagas mention. Although no one is sure about what *mösurr* wood was, the best guess is that it was bird's-eye maple. *Mösurr* is an early German word for "spotted," and bird's-eye maple is a kind of spotted wood. It has markings that resemble birds' eyes, and it has long been prized by cabinetmakers.

A larger Vinland would also solve the problem of the Skraelings. Most scholars think that the Skraelings of the sagas were Indians because they had bows and arrows, which Eskimos did not have at that time. But the Indians of Newfoundland were the Beothuks, a people who lived by hunting in the woods and collecting food along the coast. Later explorers found them a simple, shy people, who were in no way warlike. So scholars wonder whether the Beothuks could have been the Skraelings whose attacks forced the Greenlanders to give up the idea of colonizing Vinland.

These Skraelings sound more like one of the Algonquian tribes, which were widespread in eastern North America. As described later by French and English settlers, the Algonquians were skilled hunters, trappers, and fishermen. Some tribes practiced farming, and they stored corn in dome-shaped houses made of poles lashed together and covered with bark, a description that fits the wooden storehouse discovered by Thorvald's men. Algonquian tribes were often friendly in their first encounters with white settlers, coming to meet them with bundles of furs to trade or to offer as gifts. But

A Viking nail found at the Norse settlement. The Northmen were skilled ironworkers. The twelfth-century Norwegian carving shows a smith (bottom right) hammering a sword at his forge, while his assistant works the bellows.

Some people believe that this stone tower in Newport, Rhode Island, was built by Vikings. Although it is old, there is no way to be sure whether it was built by Norsemen or later explorers or early American colonists.

if they were met with hostility, they could and did fight bravely, attacking in yelling war parties and shooting arrows as they came.

Apart from what the sagas tell us, there is another reason to think that Vinland reached south into New England. In 1930 archeologists excavated the house where Karlsefni lived in Greenland after his marriage to Gudrid. In one of the rooms a lump of coal was discovered. The find surprised the archeologists, because no coal ash has ever been found in the hearths of the Greenland colonists; there is only wood ash. The coal proved to be a kind of anthracite, and this was even more surprising. No deposits of anthracite coal have ever been found in Greenland. There are none in Iceland or Norway, the two countries with which Greenland was linked by ship. There are none in eastern Canada or northern New England. This kind of anthracite occurs in only two places on the east coast of North America. Both are in Rhode Island and near the sea.

The most likely explanation of the coal is that Karlsefni sailed as far south as Rhode Island and landed. Like many other travelers, Karlsefni and his companions collected some souvenirs before sailing for home. One was a lump of coal. Perhaps others will yet be found in Greenland.

The voyages of discovery, as described in the sagas, were over by the year 1020, and by then the Greenlanders had given up the idea of starting a colony in Vinland. They were too few in number and too far from home to found a colony and hold it against the attacks of Skraelings. We know, however, that they continued to sail to Markland and Vinland for timber and furs, because they traded these goods with other countries. New World products appear on Norwegian customs lists. And the *Icelandic Annals,* which are yearly accounts of events, record that in 1347 a small Greenland ship that had been to Markland for timber was storm-driven into a harbor in western Iceland.

If the Vinland map is genuine, it shows that the Greenlanders sailed all around their huge homeland on a voyage that took them into the Arctic Ocean. And it raises a question about the two big bays shown on the map of Vinland: Did the Greenlanders explore both the Gulf of St. Lawrence and Hudson Bay?

There are people who think that the Northmen reached the very heart of North America. Their evidence is the Kensington Stone, which was found in 1898 by a Minnesota farmer who was clearing a piece of woodland. Among the roots of a tree, he discovered a rectangular piece of stone covered with strange markings. The markings proved to be a runic inscription telling of a westward

Runes on the Kensington Stone describe a two-week expedition westward from Vinland by eight Swedes and twenty-two Norwegians.

journey of Northmen from Vinland in 1362. Ever since its discovery, the Kensington Stone has been a subject of heated argument among experts on runic inscriptions. Some defend the stone as genuine. Most think it is a forgery.

There is also doubt about the significance of three rusty iron objects found in Beardmore, Ontario, in 1930. They are a Norse sword, a Norse axehead, and something that may be a rattle. There is no question about their age or origin. What is in doubt is how they got to Beardmore. Were they left there by Northmen? Or were they brought in by the very person who claimed to have discovered them?

Among the many mysteries connected with Vinland, there are several strange cases of people who suddenly disappear out of the pages of history. There is no evidence of what happened to them, but some scholars have wondered whether they became the white, bearded gods of Middle and South America. If these gods were real people and if they were northern Europeans, then this idea is as likely an explanation of who they were as any other.

The first of these people to disappear were some Irish monks who had started a religious settlement in Iceland long before the Vikings arrived. There is no record of when the settlement was started, but it must have been in the 700's or earlier. Dicuil, an Irish monk and noted scholar, wrote an excellent geography, which he finished around A.D. 825. In it, among other things, he tells of some Irish priests who, in the late 700's, set out and sailed to Iceland "at the season of greatest cold" and stayed for six months. It is clear from what Dicuil says that the priests were not setting out on a voyage of discovery but to visit a place they knew about. The route was known, as was the fact that in terms of sea and fog, winter was a good season to make the trip. And if they went to Iceland in winter to stay for some months, they obviously

Irish boat similar to the larger craft sailed by Irish priests and monks in the stormy North Atlantic. Made of simple materials (hides stretched over small branches) and almost unsinkable, such a boat could be easily repaired if damaged.

expected to find food and shelter.

Ari in the *Book of Icelanders* confirms the Irish settlement. He says that Christian priests were living in Iceland at the time the Northmen came, but that they later went away, because they did not wish to live with heathens. They left behind Irish books, bells, and croziers (the staffs carried by bishops and abbots) from which, Ari says, it could be seen that they were Irish.

Where did the priests go when they sailed away? Did they go back in the direction from which the Vikings were coming? Or did they sail westward, hoping to find the blessed isles that Irish legend placed in the western ocean?

We do not know. The priests and the people who took care of them sailed away—and out of history.

In the sagas of Vinland, however, there are references to a place called Hvitramannaland, which was thought to be a land of white men who were Irish and was said to lie westward in the sea, near Vinland. Early Icelandic sources tell of Norsemen driven by heavy gales westward across the sea to a land of white men who were Irish. In some stories the Norsemen were kept captive and later recognized by other Norsemen who had been storm-driven to Hvitramannaland.

So far, there is no way of telling whether Hvitramannaland existed or whether it is simply the Irish legend of blessed isles in a new form. But the possibility remains that the Irish priests and their people sailed westward from Iceland, stopped in Greenland, and then moved on to the west.

Some 250 years later a bishop sailed out of the pages of history. The *Icelandic Annals* record that in 1112 the Pope made Eric Gnupsson "Bishop of Greenland and nearby islands." Around 1120 the bishop set out on a visit to Vinland. The annals do not tell why he went, whether he reached Vinland, or whether he ever returned to Greenland. Was the bishop just going to look at Vinland? Were there Norsemen living there, whom he intended to visit? Did he return and write a report to the Pope that may one day be found among the records of the Vatican? Or did he never return?

The final disappearance was of the Greenlanders themselves. For some years Greenland had been a doomed colony. In the eyes of Europe, Greenland was at the world's end and of little interest. Norway fell upon hard times and lost interest in trading with a distant land. In 1367 the only ship regularly in the Greenland trade was wrecked. It was not replaced, although other ships did call in from time to time.

In 1540 an Icelander happened to sail past one of Greenland's settlements. He saw people moving about and a man lying dead on the ground. A few years later a ship out of Hamburg called at Greenland. Its captain could find no sign of life.

No one has ever known what happened to the last of the Greenlanders. Did they die of hunger and sickness? Were they killed by the Skraelings? Were they absorbed into bands of Skraelings? Were they forced to flee from Greenland because of attacks by English pirates on the settlements? If so, did they set sail for Iceland and never arrive? Or did they take what livestock and house-

*Clothing once worn by a
Greenland settler—and
preserved for hundreds of
years in the frozen
earth of a churchyard.*

hold goods they could and set out for Vinland? We know only
that sometime after 1500 the last of the colony vanished.

It is strange to think how different history would have been if
the Greenland colony had prospered and survived or if the Greenlanders had been able to establish a successful colony in Vinland.
For in the last years of the Greenland colony, other ships were
starting to sail the northern seas and coming at least in sight of
North America. And to the south the great age of exploration and
discovery had begun.

The Clues to Vinland   109

The World of Columbus

At the time of Columbus' first voyage, in 1492, the discovery of Vinland was some 500 years old. Generations of Greenlanders had explored Vinland, taken on cargoes of timber, furs, and hides, and sent some of these to Norway in trade. Vinland had been mentioned in Adam of Bremen's world geography. Its existence was well known to the people of Iceland and Scandinavia. It had probably been sighted by any number of sailors, storm-blown off course on voyages to Iceland and Greenland. And there is reason to think that by the 1480's fishermen from Bristol, England, were taking cod from the banks of Newfoundland.

Bristol at the time was England's leading Atlantic port and a place where many Norwegians had settled. Its merchants had been actively engaged in trade with Iceland since the early 1400's. And its seamen were daring, experienced, and familiar with northern seas. Old records tell us that the merchants of Bristol sent ships westward year after year and that at least some of these ships carried huge quantities of salt. These facts imply that men of Bristol had discovered a western fishing ground, where they were going to catch cod and preserve them with salt. The most likely waters were those off Newfoundland.

Even stronger evidence of the Bristol discovery lies in the voyages of John Cabot. Cabot, who was born Giovanni Caboto in Genoa, had lived in Venice. There, it is said, he worked for a merchant and had visited the Arabian city of Mecca, a trade center where spices and other riches of the East arrived by overland caravan. But very little is known about Cabot—where he had been and what he had done—before he arrived in England with his wife and sons in the late 1400's. He arrived with a globe of the world, which he had made himself, a map of the world, and an ambitious plan for sailing westward to reach the Spice Islands of the East.

The place Cabot went in England was Bristol. The king granted Cabot the right to explore in the name of England, but the ships, sailors, and money for the voyages were supplied by the merchants of Bristol.

On his first voyage to the New World, Cabot sighted land in late June of 1497 and made one landfall, probably in Newfoundland or Nova Scotia. The following year he sailed again from Bristol, taking his son Sebastian with him. He believed that on his first voyage he had reached northeastern Asia, and he intended now to follow the coast south until he reached the Spice Islands. The voyage was a long one and may have taken him as far south as Chesapeake Bay, but little is known about it. John Cabot never came back. In some unknown place, he went down with his ship.

The best account of Cabot's first voyage is in a letter written by an English merchant who was acting as an agent for the Spanish Admiralty. The letter describes in some detail what Cabot saw in the new land. It goes on to say this land is believed to be the one found earlier by men of Bristol and thought to be a mainland. And so, although England's claims in the New World started with Cabot, there is good reason to think that the fishermen of Bristol were there long ahead of him.

The men of Bristol, however, were not looking for new lands or a sea route to the East. They were looking for fish. They found a place where the waters swarmed with fish and where there was also land. But like earlier voyagers across the Atlantic, they did not understand how vast and how important that land really was.

Cabot did not understand what he had found, either. But his failure to understand was of a different kind. Cabot had drawn on the experience of men who sailed the northern seas and who knew that there was land to the west. But like Columbus he shared the belief of the most learned men of his time that land on the western side of the ocean had to be Asia. Still, it was this learned misunderstanding that spurred the great age of exploration and discovery, for the age grew out of a need to find a new route to the East.

For many years pepper, spices, silks, and other desirable things had been reaching Europe from the Far East. They were carried first by ship and then overland by caravans of camels. Bought and sold many times along the way by traders, they eventually reached the trade centers of Europe. But increasingly the overland part of the route was controlled by Muslim Turks, who held considerable land in western Asia and refused to let Christian traders travel through their lands. In 1453 the Turks seized Constantinople, a Christian city and a major trade center. With the fall of this city, the main overland route was closed. It became essential to find another route to the lands that produced the things Europeans greatly desired.

Geographers and map makers of the fifteenth century were fully aware that the earth was not flat. They knew it was shaped like a ball, and so they reasoned that there were two ways to reach the East. One was to sail around Africa and then on to India. The other was to sail westward across the ocean on a direct route to the Indies. The problem was that these routes did not show on their maps. Man's knowledge of the lands and seas that lay more than a few hundred miles off Europe was vague. Whoever attempted these routes would be sailing into the unknown.

In one country, however, a systematic attempt was under way to extend man's knowledge of the seas. This country was Portugal, a small land of farmers and fishermen that was turned into a major sea power through the work of Prince Henry the Navigator.

Greatly interested in geography, astronomy, navigation, and exploration, Henry established a center of study, where he brought together mathematicians, astronomers, map makers, and other learned men. At this same place, Sagres, he built an astronomical observatory, a naval training school, and a library. In addition, he outfitted and sent to sea numerous expeditions whose task was to explore the coast of Africa and to search the sea west of Portugal. Under Henry, ships edged their way along Africa. A westbound expedition discovered the Azores, a group of islands about a thousand miles west of Portugal, which were colonized under Henry's direction.

The work Henry had started continued after his death. By then Alfonso V was ruler of Portugal, and he soon faced a difficult decision. Africa was being explored under a private contract that was due to expire in 1474. Alfonso had to decide whether to continue exploring the African coast or to carry the search westward. It was not an easy choice. Portuguese explorers had rounded the bulge of Africa and discovered a long coastline leading south. How far south it reached, no one knew, but the route to India was proving unexpectedly long. On the other hand, expeditions

sailing several hundred miles west and north of the Azores had failed to find any signs of land.

Alfonso turned for advice to a famous scholar in Florence, Paolo Toscanelli, who was noted for his knowledge of mathematics, astronomy, and geography. Toscanelli strongly favored the idea of sailing westward, which he thought to be a much shorter way of reaching the Indies. He sent the king a chart and described two routes a ship could take. It could sail due west for 5,000 nautical miles and arrive at Quinsay (Hangchow), capital of the Chinese province of Mangi. Or it could take the second route, which included two landfalls: the island of Antilia and, 2,000 miles beyond, the island of Cipango (Japan), a land rich in gold, pearls, and precious stones, where the temples and royal residences were

Large Portuguese merchant vessels
of the early sixteenth century—
a period when both the
Portuguese and the Spanish were
expanding their overseas empires.

covered with solid gold. Thus, Toscanelli said, though the routes had not been sailed before, there were no great expanses of sea to be crossed.

In spite of this advice, Alfonso chose to go on exploring the coast of Africa. The reasons for his decision are not clear, but it is possible that his own scholars did not believe Toscanelli's chart. As we know today, Toscanelli was in great error about the size of the earth and about the distance between Portugal and Japan. The true distance is more than three times the distance shown on his chart. We do not know what size the scholars at Sagres thought the earth to be, but it was well within their powers to come close to the truth, as a Greek scholar named Eratosthenes had done around 200 B.C. Alfonso may therefore have thought that the westward voyage to the Indies was very much longer than Toscanelli imagined.

About two years after Alfonso made his decision, Christopher Columbus came by accident to Portugal. At the age of twenty-five he had sailed from Genoa as a seaman in an armed convoy that was carrying a valuable cargo to northern Europe. Off the coast of southern Portugal the convoy was attacked by French vessels, and the ship on which Columbus served was sunk. Although wounded, he managed to get ashore, and so came to Portugal. It was probably the best thing that could have happened to him.

Columbus went to Lisbon, where his younger brother Bartholomew was living and working as a chart maker. Lisbon was everything that could be wished for by an ambitious young man who was drawn to the sea. Here were the world's most knowledgeable navigators, captains who had sailed to the Azores and along the coast of Africa, a great port, a place where the trade of the Atlantic and the Mediterranean met, and a place where Columbus could read books and study languages.

Working at first with his brother, Columbus set himself to learn, studying navigation, geography, languages. He sailed in Portuguese merchant ships, learning from his fellow sailors, who were the most experienced in the world. He worked his way up to master mariner and voyaged as far as Iceland. In 1479 he married the daughter of one of Portugal's leading families. Some years later he sailed as captain on an African voyage to Guinea.

Another man might have been content to build quietly on this success, but Columbus was afire with his great dream of sailing westward to the riches of the Indies. During his years in Portugal, he had worked out his plan and he had written to Toscanelli, who replied with copies of the letter and chart he had earlier sent to Alfonso.

The chart, like all world maps of its day, showed Europe, Asia, and Africa surrounded by one huge Ocean Sea. But unlike many other scholars, Toscanelli had accepted the reports of Marco Polo, an Italian who journeyed overland to China in 1275 and who said that China was much bigger than Europeans had thought. Toscanelli had therefore stretched China eastward into the sea. That change, combined with Toscanelli's error in calculating the size of the earth, brought the Indies within easy sailing distance of Europe.

Columbus brought it even closer, for he thought the ocean was narrower than Toscanelli said. In his own calculations, Columbus made the earth 25 percent smaller than we know it to be. Then he

As the Portuguese continued to explore the coast of Africa, they finally found the route to India. Five years after Columbus' first voyage westward, Vasco da Gama reached Calicut (here shown as it looked 75 years later) by sailing eastward around the tip of Africa.

CALECHVT CELEBERRI=
MVM INDIÆ EMPORIVM.

stretched China eastward and placed Japan 1,500 miles east of China, where Marco Polo had heard it was. Making a few more corrections, he found that, according to his own chart, a voyage of 2,400 nautical miles would carry him from the Canary Islands to Japan. (Toscanelli had thought that distance to be about 3,000 nautical miles. The actual distance between the Canaries and Japan is 10,600 miles.) In terms of modern geography, Columbus expected to find Japan where our maps show the Gulf of Mexico.

In 1484 Columbus presented his plan to Alfonso's son, John II, who was by then king of Portugal. Columbus wanted backing, money, and ships. The king heard him out, but left the decision to a committee of scholars who dealt with matters of navigation and discovery. The committee turned the plan down. Perhaps they had a better idea of the distance to be covered. Perhaps they thought the African route more promising. Perhaps they thought that Columbus wanted too great a reward if he succeeded. We do not know.

In 1485, the same year that the committee turned him down, Columbus' wife died. Taking their son Diego, his chart, and his bold plan, Columbus left Portugal to try his luck in Spain. There, although Ferdinand and Isabella listened to his plan with interest, he had to wait six years for an answer and then was refused.

A dream such as Columbus' dies hard. He was about to leave for France, to present his project to the French king, when a powerful official of the Spanish court persuaded Isabella to change her mind. Columbus was four miles out of town when the queen's messenger caught up with him.

And so it happened that early in the morning of August 3, 1492, three small ships set sail from Spain under the command of Christopher Columbus. They put in at the Canaries and then sailed on a voyage that brought them to a pleasant island inhabited by people whom Columbus called Indians.

Who Discovered America?

In the history of mankind, many important things have been discovered or learned, only to be forgotten or otherwise lost, and then discovered again.

The ancient Greeks knew the true shape of the earth, and Eratosthenes came close to calculating its actual size. Yet for a very long time this knowledge was lost, and men thought that the earth was flat. By the time of Columbus, learned men had rediscovered the shape of the earth, but few, if any of them, had a realistic idea of its size. Even the idea of sailing westward around the world had occurred to people long before the fifteenth century. Strabo, a Greek geographer who died around the year 25, wrote that such a trip had been tried. It failed, he said, because the sailors became frightened and provisions ran short.

The shape and size of Africa were known and then forgotten. Around 600 B.C. Phoenician ships sailed south along the eastern side of Africa and northward along the western side, back into the

The year after Columbus died, a globe maker first used the name "America." He was honoring Amerigo Vespucci, an Italian merchant who claimed to have explored a new continent between 1497 and 1503. If Christopher Columbus had understood that the land he found was a New World, today in all likelihood there would be a North American country named the United States of Columbia inhabited by people calling themselves Columbians.

Mediterranean. Nearly 2,000 years later, Portuguese sailors, after long years of exploring, rediscovered the shape and size of Africa and rounded the Cape of Good Hope.

The Americas were, in various ways, discovered over and over again.

They were discovered by wandering hunters who happened across a now-vanished land bridge and ended by settling two continents. They were discovered later by coastal peoples who crossed the Bering Strait on purpose.

They were very probably discovered by early voyagers from Asia, and knowledge of a land across the sea seems to have lingered long after the early voyages ceased. The Vinland map was bound in with a manuscript called the "Tartar Relation," an account of a 7,000-mile mission to Mongolia made by a Franciscan friar in 1247. Near Japan on the map there is an inscription taken from the manuscript. Translated, it reads: "The Tartars affirm beyond doubt that a new land is situated in the outermost part of the world." How they knew, and whether they had visited this new land, the manuscript does not say.

The Americas were also discovered by Norsemen from Greenland, by storm-blown sailors, by fishermen, and perhaps by others whose traces have not yet been found.

If the discoveries in the northern seas had been better known, if Asian knowledge had been more widespread, then European geographers of the fifteenth century might have suspected that something lay between Europe and the East. As it was, they thought, as Strabo had, that nothing except the Ocean Sea lay between the two.

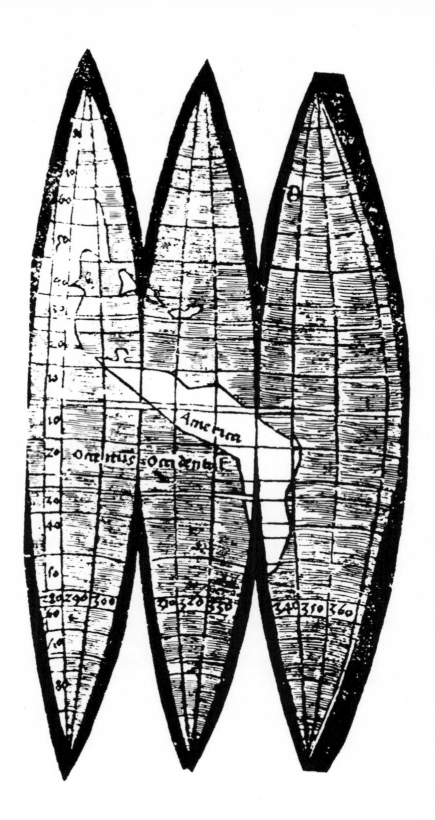

Men such as Columbus and Cabot knew what the most learned geographers thought, and so it was clear to them that when they crossed the sea and came to land, the land was Asia. It was a difficult idea for men to get out of their minds.

Perhaps the first man to suspect the truth was Peter Martyr, a tutor at the court in Barcelona who became the earliest historian of the New World. Viewing the Indians, parrots, plants, fruits, and other evidence that Columbus had brought back from his first voyage as proof of his discovery, Peter Martyr concluded that Columbus had discovered not the Indies but a new world.

Other men soon came face to face with that same truth. As a few years passed and more voyages were made, those who searched for a western sea route to the Indies discovered that the ocean was far from empty, that land stood in their way, and that on the far side of it lay still another ocean.

In their search for a way through or around the land, explorers probed and mapped the coasts of North and South America. Gradually the whole truth emerged: What they had found was a new world, made up of two great continents.

The continents were huge, the ships small, and the voyages dangerous. From the time Columbus made his first landfall, nearly 300 years passed before the outline of the New World was complete. By then large parts of the Americas had been claimed, explored, and colonized by people who were making the land theirs—and the American Revolution was three years old.

The final corner of the outline was filled in by the voyages of Vitus Bering and Captain Cook, and that corner was where it all began: at the Bering Strait, where Alaska and Siberia reach toward each other and were once joined by a bridge of land.

Who discovered America? It is not an easy question to answer. But if someone asked you, what would you say?

Selected Bibliography

Anderson, Douglas D. "A Stone Age Campsite at the Gateway to America." *Scientific American,* June 1968, Vol. 218, No. 6.

Donovan, Frank R. *The Vikings.* American Heritage Publishing Co., Inc., 1964.

Ekholm, Gordon. "The New Orientation Toward Problems of Asiatic-American Relationships." *New Interpretations of Aboriginal American Culture History,* Anthropological Society of Washington, D.C., 1955.

Estrada, Emilio, and Meggers, Betty J. "A Complex of Traits of Probable Transpacific Origin on the Coast of Ecuador." *American Anthropologist,* Vol. LXIII (1961).

Evans, Clifford, and Meggers, Betty J. "Valdivia—an Early Formative Culture of Ecuador." *Archeology,* Autumn, 1958, Vol. 11, No. 3.

Farb, Peter. *Man's Rise to Civilization as Shown by the Indians of North America from Primeval Times to the Coming of the Industrial State.* E. P. Dutton & Co., Inc., 1968.

Grosso, Gerald H. "Cave Life on the Palouse." *Natural History,* February 1967, Vol. LXXVI, No. 2.

Haag, William G. "The Bering Strait Land Bridge." *Scientific American,* January 1962, Vol. 206, No. 1.

Haynes, C. Vance, Jr. "Elephant-hunting in North America." *Scientific American*, June 1966, Vol. 214, No. 6.

Heyerdahl, Thor. *Sea Routes to Polynesia*. Rand McNally & Company, 1968.

Hibben, Frank C. *The Lost Americans*. Thomas Y. Crowell Company, 1968.

Hopkins, David M. (editor). *The Bering Land Bridge*. Stanford University Press, 1967.

Howells, William. *Back of History*. Natural History Library, 1963.

Ingstad, Helge. *Land under the Pole Star*. St. Martin's Press, 1966.

Ingstad, Helge. *Westward to Vinland*. St. Martin's Press, 1969.

Jennings, Jesse D. and Norbeck, Edward (editors). *Prehistoric Man in the New World*. The University of Chicago Press, 1964.

Jones, Gwyn. *A History of the Vikings*. Oxford University Press, 1968.

Jones, Gwyn. *The North Atlantic Saga*. Oxford University Press, 1964.

Kirk, Ruth. "The Discovery of Marmes Man." *Natural History*, December 1968, Vol. LXXVII, No. 10.

Meggers, Betty J. and Evans, Clifford. "A Transpacific Contact in 3000 B.C." *Scientific American*, January 1966, Vol. 214, No. 1.

Morison, Samuel Eliot. *Admiral of the Ocean Sea*. Little, Brown & Co., 1942.

Oxenstierna, Eric. "The Vikings." *Scientific American*, May 1967, Vol. 216, No. 5.

Sauer, Carl O. *Agricultural Origins and Dispersals*. The M. I. T. Press, 1969.

Sauer, Carl O. *Northern Mists*. University of California Press, 1968.

Skelton, R. A., Marston, Thomas E., and Painter, George D. *The Vinland Map and the Tartar Relation*. Yale University Press, 1965.

Wauchope, Robert. *Lost Tribes and Sunken Continents*. The University of Chicago Press, 1962.

For readers of *Who Discovered America?* the books by Donovan, Hibben, and Wauchope are particularly recommended, as are the articles in *Natural History* by Grosso and Kirk.

Index

About the Author

Patricia Lauber, formerly Chief Science Editor of *The New Book of Knowledge,* has written more than forty books for young readers. Her Random House titles include *The Friendly Dolphins, Your Body and How It Works, The Look-It-Up Book of the Fifty States,* and *The Planets.* A graduate of Wellesley College, she lives in New York City.

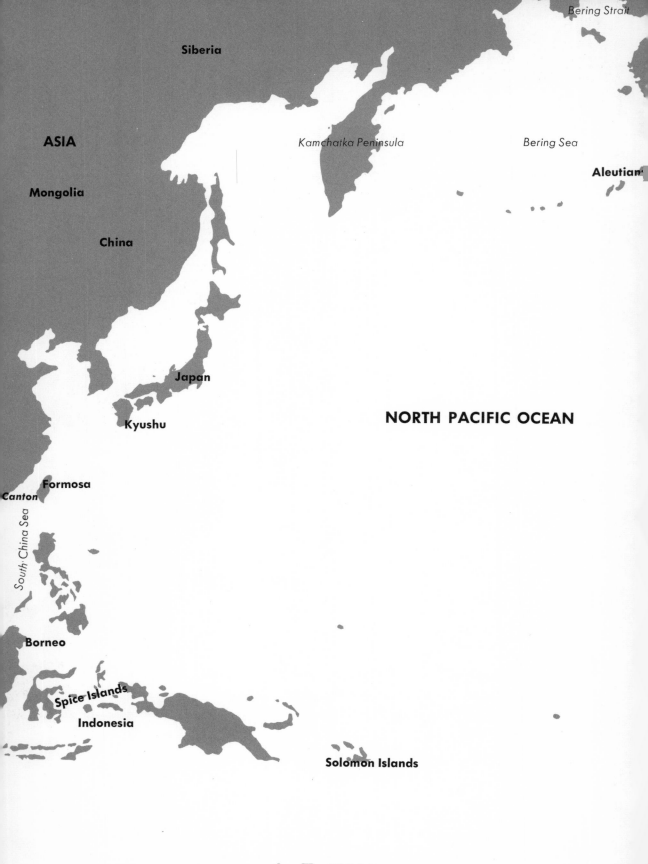

Bering Strait

Siberia

ASIA

Kamchatka Peninsula

Bering Sea

Mongolia

Aleutian

China

Japan

NORTH PACIFIC OCEAN

Kyushu

Formosa

Canton

South China Sea

Borneo

Spice Islands

Indonesia

Solomon Islands

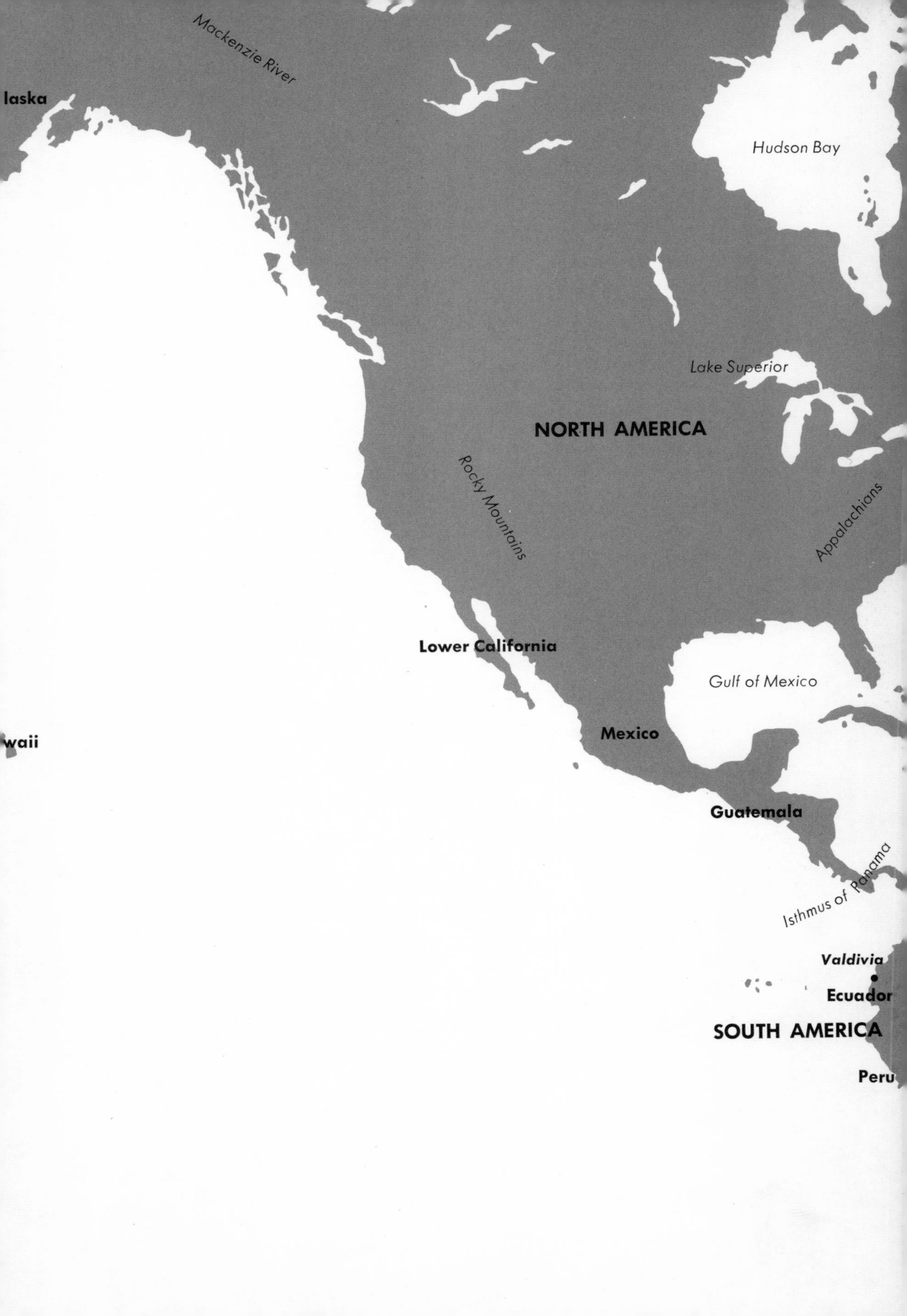

laska

Mackenzie River

Hudson Bay

Lake Superior

NORTH AMERICA

Rocky Mountains

Appalachians

Lower California

Gulf of Mexico

waii

Mexico

Guatemala

Isthmus of Panama

Valdivia
Ecuador

SOUTH AMERICA

Peru